MARRIAGE DECLASSIFIED

What Am I Getting Into?

MICHAEL R WARREN

ISBN: 0692348476
ISBN 13: 9780692348475

First Edition: January 2015

Artwork Provided by Clif Dickens

TABLE OF CONTENTS

ACKNOWLEDGMENTS

All my gratitude is owed to our Creator
who put this message in my heart.

To my wife who has been more than a blessing in her love and support for this journey. It is not enough to say that we have come a long way from our first days as husband and wife. We often discussed the possibility of having a marriage that would surpass our wildest dreams. It seems we are well on our way to that goal. I appreciate your will to be the wife that I need and deserve. It truly gives me the desire to be your champion. Your confidence in me is like none I have ever known and the best way for me to show my thanks is to get out there and win.

You have grown into a wonderful mother to our children. They have no idea how fortunate they are to be surrounded by your love each day. The way you care for them is nothing short of amazing. I love you.

To my daughters, your smiles and laughter make my heart swell with joy. Daddy is always trying to teach you important stuff like why it's necessary to wash your hands and why we should avoid those pesky black holes at the edge of the universe, because both of those things could impact your health. The truth is that I learn as much from you both by learning to live in the moment and be authentic in my feelings. My love for you knows no bounds, and it is an indescribable honor to father you both. Take your time growing up. Daddy loves you.

Thanks to all my family and friends who have cheered me along in this endeavor. This was a huge leap of faith for me to complete and it always helped to hear words of encouragement along the way.

To Marjie, thank you for all of the time and wisdom you have invested in helping me develop as a writer. What you have helped me uncover is a talent that I never knew I had and a gift that I'm ready to share. I deeply appreciate your honesty and the challenge to be a grander version of myself. God bless.

INTRODUCTION

Anyone who tells you that marriages don't have problems is selling you a dream. Yes, there will be nights when you turn your backs on each other in bed, but after that comes love. Yes, there will be decisions that require your input regardless of whether you give a damn or not, but after that comes love. Yes, there will be days when you want to disappear after a rough day with the baby, but after that comes love. Yes, you may have to come home early from a guy's night out, but what's waiting on you is love. No, you cannot see what else is out there because what you will find is not love. No, you can't just give up and quit in the face of difficulty because who then will maintain the love?

There is no razzle-dazzle in matrimony, just a simple exchange of work and reward. Put little to no love in what you do and that's what's coming out the other end. If you completely throw yourself into this relationship then what you should expect and deserve is the very same thing.

—from the Conclusion

There is no preparation for two things in this world: becoming a husband and becoming a father. I guess to some degree that is true of war, too, but I have never been a soldier. It does seem to me that a soldier goes through a significant amount of training that at least fosters some level of confidence through preparedness.

I am a husband and a father. I would like to have had some of that same preparedness.

I decided to write this book after being married for ten years and experiencing the ups and downs that marriage most certainly brings. The fundamentals that set you up for a great marriage are rarely revealed until after a couple has failed or is failing—as if these habits were some government secret. So we will declassify these principals in an effort to help couples forge a partnership that will stand up to all the challenges that await.

I am announcing up front that I chose the best partner for me. She has either matched or exceeded my effort to make our relationship a shelter and refuge from the cosmic levels of negativity that wait for you to step outside your door every morning and attempt to sabotage what you've created together. I am declaring in this book that married life **can be** rewarding, peaceful, safe and prosperous. The only problem is that there is currently no Marriage Depot or Matrimony Mart that you can stroll into on a Saturday afternoon and grab the new Marriage 2.0 off the promo rack; the fact is that you have to go out into the woods, gather materials and craft it yourself.

Marriages have been the bedrock for most cultures and communities for centuries. They have also been the driving engine for producing healthy, well-adjusted children who then grow up to raise the next generation. The institution of marriage is under attack from a lot of different angles. When you really think about it, you live in a world that profits from pain and suffering. If you are in a great relationship, that is ultimately bad for business. The more well-adjusted husbands and wives there are, the fewer night club romances there will be. What happens to industries that feed on chaos then? How many fewer pornographic sites would be visited? How much less alcohol would be guzzled in the driveway in hopes of preparing one's mind for coming home to "deal with the family?" How many more meals at home would be had with Papa at the head of the table waiting to hear how everybody's day went?

This culture of denial and self-medication is putting money in somebody's pocket. This is not a book aimed at businesses profiting from pain and suffering, but the markets are oversaturated with ways to avoid your real problems by convincing you that there can be reward with no work, and problem solving is just a dollar away. If you think healthy marriages aren't under attack, go up to the nearest mountaintop and shout out, "I love being married!" and see how tomatoes and rocks get hurled at you.

I won't bother you with a bunch of charts and data to impress you with statistics on marriage. The realities shared in this book are based on the observations of experienced married men. This is collective wisdom that I am sharing based on conversations and interviews with dozens of men. Their observations are real, tangible and can be seen and heard in exchanges pretty much every day in stores, offices and even at church. These topics manifest themselves in stray comments like, "I just can't get Bob to do squat around here," or "The old lady got me doing XYZ."

Hearing and seeing people living under this cloud of discontent would lead a single man to think that anybody who gets married has just signed his death warrant and turns into this mindless drone being controlled by his puppet-master wife. Who could blame a man for being hesitant to throw himself to the wind for an institution he knows little about and, frankly, that doesn't get much verbal reinforcement. What you don't hear enough about is marriage as a good strategy for one's life.

You don't have to be a clinical professional to see that marriage holds the power to bring about an evolution of a person that is both potent and lasting. There are few things in this world that can make that claim, so if you're shopping down another aisle then, "buyer beware."

I am a 37-year-old husband, father and spiritual leader of my household. The intent of this book is to shine a little light on the much-overlooked "process" of building a marriage. There is a process for all things in this world, whether it be organic or mechanical, in order for them to function as desired or to be able to predict their specific outcome. In most cases, when you buy a product or enroll in a class there is a specific order in which things are done. You believed the marketing and anticipate that what you bought will ultimately meet your need. The expectations are similar to when you stay up late at night and buy those "left-handed nun chucks" from that crazy infomercial, and quickly find out they are no more awesome than the ambidextrous set you own. Instantly, you want your money back; and so it seems with relationships.

Troubled relationships all seem to share a root problem: unpreparedness. That common root fosters comments like, "I didn't know who I was really dealing with," or, "I saw signs of trouble or conflict but I didn't ask questions." Like most folks, I have made my share of dumb decisions with the opposite sex as a result of being extremely selfish; but I did pull some valuable lessons from those situations.

In fact, too many relationships accelerate way too damn fast for people to realize what path they are setting themselves on. A lot of marriages are in bad shape, from the outside looking in, so imagine what they are like inside. We all have seen the couple eating dinner together who are looking around not saying a single word to each other. Is it possible they are having a little spat? Maybe, or it could be they are on a forced date night but ultimately have nothing to say to each other. I would also highlight the old man in the department store whose wife has dragged him into the lingerie section to sit in *the chair*. You know which one I'm talking about; the one right by the fitting room where everyone can see you on display as either a supportive spouse or a **sucker**.

These daily and common examples can seem depressing, but I challenge you to keep two things in mind as you move through the book and your relationship: "the power of choice" and "the process you follow." You can have a *great* marriage by making *great* choices. Choosing to put your spouse before others, choosing to pay close attention to each other and choosing not to be the normal couple will set you up for success. Those *great* choices are then followed with *great* actions that have to be rooted in *great* habits. This will lead you to the outcome you so desire and deserve.

Love and relationships can be a tough investment but I have had enough victories and seen enough return on my investment to believe, without a doubt, it is worth the effort and a hell of a lot better than lying to yourself about not needing somebody. We all need and want somebody who brings out and values our true selves; we just need to be smart about how we bring those people into our lives. There is an old but good saying, "If you keep doing what you're doing; then you are going to keep getting what you got."

Imagine marriage as a remote control for your High Definition TV. In most homes, you will find a large flat screen hung on a wall for all to see, and most people will comment on the size and the picture. With this TV comes a remote that has more than 20 different function buttons. However most of us only use the **power, volume** and **channel** buttons. Few of us actually read the manual to understand what the other 17 buttons do or how they will enhance our viewing experience, so we settle for our TV just being BIG or Rich in Pixels. Big Deal! Everybody has one. What would happen if someone from the "tech support" walked you through those 17 buttons in an effort to give you more functionality out of your TV? Bam!! Now you can do everything from surf the web to reply to your buddy's video call coming from your smartphone. How much more excited would you be about your TV? How less likely would you be willing to trade it for a bigger and brighter one that just had a **power, volume** and **channel** button on it?

A high-definition union can't just start out with an "I DO" and then reach its full potential with you using the same three buttons you previously used, with no expectations of a greater and more meaningful relationship (20 buttons). There is serious work to be done that ranges from great to not-so-fun; but if you honor the full scope of your vows you will have the TV that all your friends keep inquiring about. So if you are about to say," **I do**," then make the choice "**To do**."

I hope you find this book entertaining, inspiring and a bold incentive to veer away from what "everybody else is doing." I challenge men to stand up and stretch yourselves into the spouses you can and should be. I challenge women to appreciate the good in your man and embolden him to seek out "his best," so that he can serve you and his family and be an example to others.

I hope you find love, purpose and peace at the end of the path you have chosen.

My name is Michael Warren, and I gave up the gamesmanship, lies and chaos in order to gain certainty, truth and harmony.

My first question is: Will you?

Chapter I
YOU DO MATTER

If ever there was a simplistic way of explaining some of the wonders and beauty of being in a committed long-term relationship, it is that you as a person and a spirit matter. This potent concept anchors you in a solid bedrock, providing a foundation for everything from your love to your pain. This concept is critical to a marriage because this journey with your spouse will expose both of you for everything that you are, both good and not so good. All of your insecurities and hang-ups will be on full display as his/her "issues." The negative things that you have carried around all your lives are about to go through an airport-security-like screening process before you can get to your destination, which is harmony with your spouse. Couples should support each other in realizing the broken parts of their loved one, thus beginning a healing that only a husband or wife can provide.

The desire to be part of the healing is first vocalized, then acted on. For example a husband may say to his wife, who has been marginalized all her life, "I am going to celebrate you in all that you do." Or a wife may say to her husband, who had no father, "You are who I chose to lead my family, and even if you had no example to follow I'm going to love and support you as you figure it out." There are countless ways to demonstrate this to a loved one, and these acts should be at the core of your relationship.

Getting married would certainly be much easier if your marriage license came with an owner's manual and a warranty guide, but since it doesn't most couples find themselves submerged in a mound of challenges and opportunities. It would seem like a being a dad on Christmas eve as you sit waist-high in a pile of toy parts trying to put everything together based off the picture on the box. At some point frustration beats out patience and he shouts "honey have you seen the directions?"

Brokenness

Brokenness is part of marriage. There is not a single person who has made it to adulthood without a few emotional scars. Pain is usually inflicted by a partner who is equally broken; it would be similar to a two-headed supermodel arguing with herself about who has the better body. When you are one, pain effects both. This is not meant to be gloomy, but when you enter marriage, it is under the drunken influence of love. Passion skews your vision to see only the shiniest parts of your spouse. You see things like great beauty, strength or even humor and a kind smile. It isn't until a few months later that you are introduced to insecurity, emotional weakness and selfishness. How do you deal with this? Sadly, most people don't deal with this until they find themselves at a marriage counselor or in divorce court, when all the chaos and turmoil have reached a fever pitch and everything is boiling over for all to see.

Oddly enough, there is a blessing in this brokenness because it means that through your union you have arrived at a place where you can begin healing from your past, resolute in your NOW and emboldened about your future.

Stay Engaged

It's critical for couples to take on this task of understanding what it means to matter in a marriage. The essence of mattering would suggest that it means different things on different days.

In my home it could mean on Thursday, my wife hands over responsibility of something she normally does because she trusts that I'm capable of doing it in *my own way*. On Sunday, it could look like her ushering our very loud and vibrant kids out of the bonus room because the Green Bay Packers are playing and I can't hear the game. On the flipside, for my wife it may play out as me helping her do the girls' hair, which takes "*forever*" in hopes of cutting her work in half. Or it can be as simple as pausing in my day to simply tell her what a wonderful mother she has become. She deserves to hear and see these things. We both do. Why? Because we both matter.

As a man, you need to know that your joys and pains matter to your wife and that they stay on her radar so that she can be that refuge and catalyst for your continuing growth. Men rarely admit any weaknesses or vulnerabilities, so when they find themselves in a relationship where emotions start rolling and let down their guard, all their "stuff" gets aired out. Sometimes, it may be to their wives' dismay. Women may be taken aback by this cascade of feelings from a dude who has adopted three or four hobbies as a way of shirking responsibilities at home, or from a guy who is non-confrontational by nature and lets her steamroll over him. Most guys have a way of hiding behind something else in order to disguise a weakness or insecurity. Often, men would rather walk out of the house or flip a table over than admit their fragile egos have been damaged.

Train to Be a Champion
Husbands should be seeking out exactly what their wives' joys and pains are so that they can acknowledge the existence of those elements in her life. You thus declare to her that you're willing to play out your part in the solution, whether that be standing up and being more aggressive about a matter or the reverse, which is simply sitting back and shutting up. This action will speak volumes into her world. It shouts that she matters and you are putting love and healing in action. That will get the "fires burning."

The way that you perform in a competition or evaluation is a direct result of how you practiced. When we make it a common practice to show our spouse that they matter it sets you up to be a champion in other facets of the relationship. This regiment can start out with one gesture a week and increase over time. Before you realize it you have made it a habit to acknowledge your partner without any concerted effort. The chapters ahead will reveal opportunities to "matter more" to each other and what this can mean for your unions.

You Matter: Declassified

- Marriage doesn't work without YOU

- None of you got a blueprint or cheat sheet for marriage

- The emotional arena is new for a lot of guys so patience is required

- Spouses need to be each other's champions

- You can heal the broken parts of each other if you know they exist

- Marriage is not a one man show

- You can't overdose on encouragement

Chapter 2
MAN ABANDONED

One of my dreams growing up was to be a fighter pilot. I would read magazines and watch movies like *Top Gun* and the Iron Eagle series to get amped up. I probably dated myself with these references. That dream has never gone anywhere. It just got nudged further and further into the back of my mind and replaced with more immediate and tangible things like career and family. Still, if I ever got the chance to fly in a military fighter jet, it would be my own personal Christmas.

I mention my dream because I believe these stashed dreams contribute to a period when a man takes inventory of his accomplishments and makes efforts to recapture past glory or embark on that thing he never got a chance to do.

Being Human

A man tries to find himself when he feels that he somehow got lost or abandoned in everyone else's world. How can a man possibly be abandoned, you ask? After all this is a man's world. Right? We have been collectively bamboozled! We bought a big screen TV off the street and when we got it home and opened it up, the box was full of bricks. We've somehow told ourselves that to be married you have to trim the fat in your personality and soul in order to fit in this box called "husband" or "wife." It's simply not true. Nor is it good for you. A good marriage should actually reinforce and amplify who you are as a person. Only through the spiritual and emotional conflict that marriage puts you through can you realize that potential. Our cultural philosophy requires husbands to be good providers, protectors and overall managers of the family unit, which is true. Missing is the glaring reality that we often forget to be "human" along with it. What does being human mean? In essence, being human means being both flawed and gifted. You have needs that need to be met on many different levels. You also have visions and ambitions for personal advancement that need to be fed. When these little flames are extinguished completely in order to focus solely on everyone else, it can lead to a miserable existence even when those around you are prospering. You need to know as a man that your wife acknowledges your need to feel appreciated and loved as much as you need to be fed and made love to. Sure most guys will take the last two in a heartbeat, but you need to quit denying your larger needs. You need it and you deserve it. So quit the charade and acknowledge your unmet needs. Acknowledge also the need for patience and understanding until you can "get on your feet" on this level. Then once you are on your feet; start moving them.

An Ocean of Emotion
Our culture perpetuates the lie that women are more emotional than men. There is validity to that statement but it does not recognize that men have the same emotions; they have just typically been undernourished or frankly beat out of them as young boys. Some control of emotions is necessary for survival in dangerous situations like battle or intense conflict. You can't just drop your sword and start crying because the enemy has more soldiers on their side. While that is an extreme case, you need to examine all the knee-jerk reactions you have had in your past because of hurt feelings or disappointment.

How many bullies have emerged out of children who have had aggression thrust upon them at a young age with no vocabulary to express that they are being damaged by it? Instead little Brutus is out taking lunch money and extorting test scores from the valedictorians in his math class. How many cowards have been created because they were unable to express fear or uncertainty to an elder who could then tell them it is okay to be frightened; they can rise above this and conquer their fear and then be celebrated because they did just that? How many "womanizers" have been created because their connection to their mother wasn't as it should have been, so they carry on in life looking for that love in the laps of random women? All the while, they are lying and deceiving those who perceived their relationships as genuine. How many liars have been created because they couldn't express on an emotional level: "Hey, am I good enough as I am?" How many slick stories have they told to convince people that they are, in fact, good enough or smart enough or even rich enough to be desired? That dude needs to know from his wife that the "truth" really is okay. So what if he doesn't have money, status, education or employment. Those are tangible things that he can attain. The one thing he can't get through lying is the one thing he desires the most: acceptance of the authentic him.

There has been a collective abandonment of men's emotional needs in our society, and we continue to reap the rotten fruit of this behavior every single day. Men all over this country are turning to drugs, violence and sex as a means to either avoid or retreat from their emotional experiences. Then they lash out in some other fashion to get attention.

Understanding Who You Are
Husbands and dads are regularly portrayed as bumbling idiots whose wives have to manage them like a child. Homer Simpson is an archetype. While there probably are some real life Homers, it's not an epidemic. When it comes to things like being handy around the house or tinkering with things, it's engrained in the male DNA to make an effort to solve problems or improve things with or without the technical background to do so or not. So a husband's car restoration project should not be threatening to a marriage unless it is absorbing too much money and too much time while other things in the household suffer. One can only assume that the project was jointly discussed and expectations set as far as cost and time of completion. The opposite of this may play out in a buddy of yours funneling money into an old rusted out '67 Chevy parked in his friend's backyard while his wife thinks the "extra" money is going to feed kids in an impoverished fishing village on the other side of the globe.

Men still have dreams and ambitions above and beyond taking care of their families. Lending support to them is an opportunity for a wife to acknowledge her husband's wants being achievable, once home responsibilities are met.

The role of "Man" only encompasses a portion of our total being. A man's role and responsibilities can be fully realized and still have a guy feeling unfulfilled in his life. A reason for this could be that he may be an artist or a musician with an ear for sounds but no technical ability to get a melody out of his head and onto paper. Men have an opportunity to visit who they are as a spirit in this world and figure out how to channel that gift into this realm. I have learned now that my thirst for knowledge and an appreciation for all people helps me find reward in teaching. Have you answered that question in your own life? Who am I, and what is my gift? Surely the answer is grander then "I'm a man."

A husband can help his wife learn his internal makeup when sizing him up as a father and a provider by sharing with her all the things that are important to him. He is also a "person with his own dreams," who will provide for his wife and family in addition to, not in lieu of, his own ambitions. We need husbands in this country who are happy not only because their wives' and kids' dreams are being nurtured, but because theirs are as well.

Man Abandoned: Declassified

- Seize the opportunities that life gives you and have no regrets when reflecting on your life

- Recognize and embrace your humanity

- Being a man is just the starting point in your evolution as a person

- Stop denying the existence of emotion in your life

- Understand who you are as a spirit and what your gift is

Chapter 3
LET'S WAKE UP AND CATCH UP

Historically marriage has often been used as a conduit for consolidating power in kingdoms and in societies in order to promote some level of consistency. Arranged marriages were the norm for this reason; however, in this current age the primary driver for people marrying is love or at least what we think is love. Not every person gets married because of love. Loving someone is a process that is ongoing and has to be maintained. How can you love for a year or two and call it quits when you get bored? You may "love" what a person can do or provide for you and all the while there may be no deep connection. That doesn't just happen by default.

We need to wake up and open our eyes to what is happening around us. The nature of relationships has changed because the world has changed. Some of these changes tie into advances in technology that has made some traditional roles or institutions obsolete. Women have made tremendous contributions to the workforce in numbers that grow yearly. If you look back two generations, the primary breadwinners were men. Guys did all the building, harvesting, fighting and dying if need be. The old model worked, but it was simple and didn't allow for men to be as engaged as husbands and fathers as we can be today. Now look at what all of us are able to accomplish in the twenty-first century through use of technology. Robots build everything; one piece of farm equipment does the work of fifty men; and women have also taken up arms in the military. So the question may come up: Why does a woman need a man? In regards to basic survival, men aren't needed for the same things that they were years ago. This may sound depressing, but unlike most machines that have had their day, men have the ability to evolve if they so choose—to stay in step as the world changes.

Through your personal evolution, you are confronted with the fact that as a man you are capable of contributing so much more to your family than food, muscle and a paycheck. This was the old way of being present in the family structure. As long as a man brought home money, lifted heavy stuff around the house and was servicing his wife regularly, he was doing his job. This arrangement worked out, but it came at a price. How many of you can tell the story of dad being at work from sunup to sundown to provide for his family only to realize that you never really "knew" him or had any "human" moments with him? There are countless examples of kids seeing their father only in passing as he was on his way somewhere else. He might pause just long enough to give a pat on the head or a quick Confucian-like tidbit of wisdom about homework or brushing teeth, with his presence elevating the mundane to the sacred.

Different as the almost absentee father-providers were to the current norm, there was still a family solidarity and two people to support each other. This book is aimed at getting families back to that solidarity. The changes in that area are creating social pressures. All around you, the effects of single-parent homes can be seen. The single parent and children are being robbed of the home life everyone deserves. Any parent who has had a spouse out of town for several days knows the stress of trying to do it all. There is no such thing as relaxing when you are picking up, dropping off, cooking, cleaning and doing bath time. Don't you get tired even thinking about it? Parents and kids deserve an environment where there is love and balance, and while it is possible with only one adult, it is certainly much more difficult.

A Foundation for Love

Currently, we are being polarized and distracted by a heated debate about what marriage is and who gets to participate. This book is not going to mount that political platform. This book is about two people in a marriage and how they can make it work. Because marriage is under scrutiny, currently there is an opportunity to look at what marriage has been versus what it can be. The U.S. Census Bureau published some staggering stats from 2013 that the average marriage rate was 6.8 per 1000 of the population. However the average divorce rate was 3.6 per 1000. That is slightly over half of all marriages in the United States fail and that is just the official numbers not including the folks who have checked out or are sleeping in separate bedrooms. It is evident that it is the people and not the institution itself that are to blame. You can serve your relationships best by being honest about what you hope the marriage will bring and learning early on what behaviors and attitudes will be useful. This can be done by establishing a vision for your marriage. There is a verse in the bible that says you would be foolish to build a house on top of sand because it has no stability and is subject to the winds and rains (Matthew 7:26). This is not what we want our marriages to rest on. Foundations that stand up against time are a direct result of hard work and careful planning. The next time you are at a concert enjoying the show, realize that someone spent days building the stage. It took knowledge, time and energy. So does marriage.

When I evaluate my first couple of years of marriage I realize I was completely unprepared for what this union requires. I found myself in a "now what?" mind frame. I didn't realize that I needed to start demonstrating ability to lead a family; so I just kept on with my routine. My wife was waiting for me to jump into action and work together to build our kingdom. It was almost like some freaky *Alice in Wonderland* trip down into the rabbit hole when all I could see was this small opening. When I went through it, I quickly realized I was in a different universe. Look around and there's an unassuming tree, at least until it turns around and starts singing and tap dancing. You are not outside Wonderland anymore—you are in it. It demands that you think of others before yourself and that you strive to be completely honest.

Honesty Reigns Supreme

Telling the truth is probably one of the toughest things to do because we don't want to cause pain or hurt to our lover. Yet we don't want to keep suffering in silence, either. So what do we do about it? It is essential that we understand our differences and how they can be both a blessing to our marriage and an outright annoyance. If you hate what your partner cooks then you should let her know in a responsible way and from there be part of a solution to a new meal lineup. Will she be mad? Yes, but she will also be informed and won't waste her time cooking the steamed Cheerio and beet casserole that you've been feigning excitement about. Pain from a bruised ego only lasts a little while, but a joy built with an underpinning of love and honesty can endure for a lifetime.

There is also a spiritual component in a relationship that you should nurture however you choose to express or identify the divine. The spiritual energy in a relationship is as important as any other component. It provides another level of synchronization. There will surely be tests and trials on your marriage. If this area is strengthened, it can only help keep it together and be a refuge from any misfortune.

When you connect selflessly on these various levels such as honesty, integrity and shared faith, cooperation becomes natural. Cooperation is one of the hardest lessons to learn because you have to get out of your own way. That is tragically difficult in a culture like ours which encourages extremes of self-absorption. Most people wake up and dash off into their days with little to no consideration for anything or anyone that isn't on their to-do list. Nevertheless, countless couples make it work and our communities and country are better served when this is the case. Just think about a child who has been around both masculine and feminine energy and witnessed the cooperation in setting guidelines and codes of behavior, leading to an overall harmony in the home. What will that child bring into the world? What would a million more like him or her bring into this world?

Wake Up and Catch Up: Declassified

- Our society is changing and men must adapt to the new environment

- Take a good look at the foundation on which your marriage rests

- Men have so much more to offer their families than the traditional breadwinner role if they allow themselves to develop

- Be a student of your relationships, find what is useful and discard what isn't

- Be truthful and courageous as you prepare for marriage

Chapter 4

THE ENGAGEMENT PERIOD, BLOWN OPPORTUNITY

Let's assume that now your dream girl and you are on the same page for the most part. Whether you took the traditional path and asked for permission for your wife's hand from her family or skipped that part and eloped, the first several months have probably been the biggest blown opportunity in most marriages. The period between the engagement and the wedding is filled with a lot of work. Don't miss this opportunity to work together. The groom's participation gets missed in a majority of wedding plans.

It is a time that can seem to take forever as the bride takes off on a round-the-world tour of bridal shops, caterers, florists and the best wedding planner available to argue with. I almost forgot about getting a DJ for the reception, someone with a great passion for music and a personality that can get any party started and that person would be your uncle. He used to throw down back in the day and he would be glad to MC your function if he could just figure out how to get his records into the CD player.

Getting Involved
This is the first major project that you two will work on together. Through this process you will both find out a lot about each other, including your respective

levels of patience and selfishness. Selfishness is natural to humans, but it is highly ingrained when you consider the wedding celebration is about the bride and her girlhood dream being realized. A future groom should understand that as you move forward in life there will be multitudes of things that don't have anything to do with you or directly benefit you, but your input and participation will be appreciated if not required, depending on the task.

Women should be aware that most men see this process as something to be avoided. They dodge with statements like, "Just let me know what time to show up at the church and I'll be there," as they swig beer and chuckle with their buddies. Understanding that men are purposeful and task-oriented will help women share ownership of their joint celebration. His buy-in may be surprising when he is given a meaningful role. In recent times, men are becoming more hands-on with their families. Families and society as a whole will benefit from this participation. So fellas, if you've got an idea or suggestion, offer it, but do so delicately because this is her dream. Nonetheless, your input does matter. Your wedding day will be a topic of conversation for the rest of your life and you don't want to have any regrets or ill will because you didn't have a say or you didn't mention that you wanted something.

Typically, brides and their mothers get consumed by the event with everything else falling to the wayside, and with good reason. It would be akin to a guy wanting to own a bar and grill. His focus on customer experience would surely drive him to only get his supplies from reputable food and beverage vendors and not some guy in a back alley selling spirits and expired snack cakes out of a rusty van. You will have to exercise great patience and understanding throughout this process and allow for the whole range of emotions, because they will be all over the place, depending on the demands of the day.

For example, she may want to get married in a cathedral that has grand architectural features and seats 300. Unfortunately the cost of feeding 300 could be $6,000. That's fine, except that you have 3,000 people coming and $1,000 to spend. Here is where the critical thinking as a couple comes into play because now you will have to balance out your wife's desires with your financial reality (not to say that it isn't often the other way around, but we're talking balance here). After evaluating the numbers again, you may find that the French chef and the harpist are budget busters. With that being said, maybe you should try to track down that guy with the van mentioned earlier and see how much his deposit is. (Now where did we put that napkin...I mean his business card?)

It's schooling in compromise. So maybe you bypass the cathedral and go to another location or you sacrifice your photography budget and tell everyone to bring their camera phones to splurge on *the perfect church*.

It's an unlikely scenario, of course (unless that made a light bulb go off, then in that case it's dead serious). In most cases you will channel thousands of dollars toward your perfect day. Your positions on spending will be front and center. Wedding-day veterans can offer some strong insight. Whether you have a $1,000 or a $100,000 budget, please direct your money in the best places for maximum return. Six months after your wedding no one is going to remember the color of the ribbon that was tied around a flower arrangement in the corner, or the fact that the silk was extracted from an endangered silkworm from Tibet and cost you $500 per half inch and you bought two rolls. Nobody is going to remember the music playing in the lobby while people were waiting to be seated, so no need to pay Beyoncé $100,000 to record a special song for that moment called, "Waiting."

Guests will absolutely remember if the food was good or not. They will remember if they had to pay for drinks at the bar, and they will certainly remember the flower girl and ring bearer.

There will be a ton of things to coordinate that seem so important when you are planning but, truthfully, the bride misses half of the ceremony and you will be so emotionally spun up that when you complete the night and get back to the room you won't have any stamina to make passionate love your new spouse—well maybe you could stash an energy drink under your pillow.

When the party is over the only thing you will have to take with you into your days together are your pictures and videos, so spend your money there. If the groom wants to come down the aisle dressed like a Spanish conquistador carried on the backs of recently defeated foes chanting "Oh wee oh! Yo ah!" then after you've secured a great photographer, I say do it.

Seeking Good Counsel

There is another opportunity that couples miss out on: getting real and meaningful premarital counseling and not just the two little rinky-dink sessions that most states require. If that's what you were going to do, be warned that you will be setting yourself up for blindness and failure. With such poor preparation, it is no wonder that there are so many failed marriages in the U.S. People don't take time to understand what they are getting into. It is almost like a tattoo that you can never get removed. If you get drunk and get some ink work done on your forehead that says "Forehead" then you will go through life looking like an idiot. Instead you would think about the design and the meaning behind the art. You would probably go into more than one shop and see the artist's prior work, instead of hiring that overly anxious guy across the street in the shop with no customers.

The way our society values rights that require previous instruction was one of the many reasons this book was written. Before you get a driver's license to pilot half a ton of metal at high speeds, you have to go through a driver's education program that can take weeks of learning and time behind the wheel. To carry a deadly firearm around in public only takes about $200 and an eight hour period of class or range time. You can do it in a day. But to get married—to link up with someone and operate as a unit within community that will impact others directly or indirectly for let's say the next thirty to fifty years—two two-hour sessions ought to do it, right? Wrong. All these things have a certain level of impact on our day-to-day experiences. Take driving, for example. Who hasn't poked along in the fast lane for miles behind someone doing 56 miles an hour with their left blinker on? How about the guy who volunteered to help his buddy move a dresser, TV and water heater using his Volkswagen Beetle and a roll of duct tape? And this dude took the same training class you did. Yet people are prepared to enter marriage poking along with blinkers on and slapping on duct tape instead of doing things properly. For an arrangement that you are entering for the rest of your life, you probably want to invest a little bit more than four hours. It is odd that we require a lesser amount of training in something that has a more tremendous economic, social and political impact than little Bobby who wants to take his parents' old Honda Civic to the mall. I know firsthand how important strong unions are. My family lived in one zip code that statistically had few households where there were two incomes, few registered as Mr. and Mrs. and few schools that were performing. When we moved to a different zip code that had the opposite of the first, the quality and amount of target marketing we got were polar opposites. Why? Because business and political groups know that in areas where there is a stable household with two incomes and better education, there is a larger amount of money to be solicited for a longer period of time. Kind of makes you think doesn't it? It should.

You Play How You Practice
Any project or relationship you start should be well thought out and resources made available to ensure progress and, ultimately, success. When you are going through this engagement period with your fiancé, do your best to make yourself available to each other throughout, even if you are not physically there. There will be a ton of decisions to be made and this would be the best time to learn how to support each other. Call it an Advanced Placement class for marriage. Believe me you will need this skill early and often as your union develops.

This chapter reminds me of one of my high school football coaches and his colorful spin on wisdom and motivation. If you were involved in team sports in school, then you know where I'm going with this. Coach used to tell us, "If you put a penny in, then you get a penny out." He meant that if you half-ass your way through anything in life you will get exactly what you put into it; sometimes nothing and sometimes everything. Coaches can impact people's character and help their trajectory in life. When my football coach decided to discipline my buddies and me one day for horsing around in the weight room, he told us to "take a lap" in our shorts and t-shirts during a frigid January in rural Oklahoma. After realizing this old fart wasn't playing around, we pointed out, "It's snowing outside, Coach." He replied swiftly, "Damn it, Warren! I don't care if it's ass-high to a ten-foot giant. Take a lap!" Well, my buddies and I took that lap around the track in the cold. As I have evaluated my past relationships, it has become obvious to me that due to my immaturity and selfishness I ultimately "took a lap" there as well.

The Engagement Period: Declassified

- Take the opportunity to be included in the wedding preparations

- Have no regrets about your decisions after the wedding is over. If it's going to be important later, it should be important now

- This is your crash course in compromise

- Find some solid pre-marital counseling and don't be afraid to ask tough questions

- What you put in this preparation is exactly what will come out the other end

Chapter 5

THE TRUST BUCKET

One of the most critical and fragile elements in our marriages is trust. It is one of the fundamental things you offered when you proposed. So much of your commitments and expectations for each other depend on the trust element. Trust allows you to do everything from confidently delegating family responsibilities to sharing a deep secret. It ties right into your dependability, which will be needed throughout your marriage. If wives throw up a deep pass under pressure, then husbands need to be at dead sprint to catch it in the end zone.

Credit or Debit?

There lies a process that manages the good faith and credit in every relationship. I have affectionately named it the Trust Bucket. There is no need for a grand or complex title because it is a very simple mechanism. Much like a discreet black hose under the hood of every car— whether it is luxury or economy class—if that hose comes loose, the car comes to a halt.

The importance of the bucket is that it behaves much like a bank account, with the ability to handle deposits or debits at a moment's notice. The currency used is a token of your own making. You can't buy these tokens anywhere, and there is no credit to borrow against. You have to actually fashion these by performing in your relationship in a sound and responsible manner. These tokens should be held with a high level of regard because of their exclusivity. If this sounds like a precious stone or metal then you are off the mark because you can find those in retail locations in any city. Your tokens are unique and therefore priceless.

What Am I Entrusted With?
When you got engaged and pledged your undying love and commitment to your lover you indirectly asked for her trust; you promised you would be by her side through anything. For that pledge, you got a "starter token," just for opening the account. From here, the opportunities to earn or lose tokens unfolds in the most grand and minor situations. This puts your reliability on display. Following are some examples of how trust levels sway in your marriage almost on a moment by moment basis.

A very dear friend shared a scenario with me that highlighted how fragile trust can be at times. Let's say a husband has been tasked with fixing a leaky toilet and changing out a light bulb in the basement stairway. After weeks of inaction and no progress on said items, the formerly patient wife now becomes irritated and begins to bring into question his ability to handle things. She may think to herself: "If he can't take care of a toilet and light bulb, how can I trust him with greater things like a baby or protection from a zombie apocalypse?"

A woman's need for physical security can't be overlooked; when she takes a husband she has to know that this man will be able to protect her in the event that she is in harm's way. Better yet she needs to believe he will have enough wisdom to avoid putting her or the family in a position to be harmed in the first place. This could play out in a scenario where a man and his family are at a public park enjoying a spring day when a group of suspicious fellows come into the area, who are intoxicated on alcohol or testosterone. Either way they are poised to spoil everyone's good time. They may begin shouting obscenities or begin broadcasting some chaotic intentions. The wife sees the aggression and doesn't want her family to be harmed or exposed to vulgarity. The husband has a choice to round up the crew and move on or stay put and wait for a clash that will surely come. As confident as guys are when it comes to conflict, there are times when a man can see trouble a mile away and should consider family safety over proving that his right hook is formidable. The wife will see this strategic move and find some relief that the male ego took a back seat to the family's security. Ultimately, she will know that she is safe in his hands.

Trust also comes into play in scenarios dealing with fidelity and relationships with the opposite sex. Both men and women flirt with the edges of inappropriate relationships. When you wed, you told each other that your bodies and minds were sacred to each other. This can't possibly be the case if either of those things are being loaned out on some level. Life has a million things for us to worry about, but infidelity shouldn't be one. Women need to know that you can conduct yourselves properly and not leave the door open for a very poor choice to be made. When you leave home to go just about anywhere there are choices that have to be made regarding the other gender to maintain your marital integrity. Little things like lunch with a coworker or phone calls after business hours can be open to interpretation and cause the trust to be compromised if things even "look" a certain way. It's important to be aware of what you are broadcasting when you interact with others. My wife and I came up with a simple solution: if you wouldn't do it while I was standing there, then you shouldn't do it in my absence. This may sound harsh, but what it does is remove as much doubt as possible. This in turn will give your loved one the relief and security that your affections are exclusive.

Handle with Care

Then there is emotional trust. This reaches down to the core of who you are in your marriage. The ability to be authentic in a moment of joy or pain is critical. There is a huge disconnect between men and women on this element, partly because of inadequate communication. Picture a fat rat and a rattlesnake passing each other in a tight hallway. Somebody better say "pardon me" or there is going to be a misunderstanding. Women need to know that when they are having an emotional moment, their spouses can be that quiet port away from rough waters, where they are able to complete the emotion and not be judged or patronized.

Men on the other hand need to understand how important it is to be emotional with their wives. This is tough because most men weren't shown how to do this. When they do try to express it, it may not come out right.

23

This is where men need their wives' patience. If a man feels unappreciated or intimidated, he should be able to trust his wife to receive that and validate his experience. After all, they are in this for life, so they might as well get this right. Otherwise, the husband will face years of repressed emotions that manifest themselves in some other possibly problematic behavior. In truth wives want their husbands to tell them what's going on so they can help or just listen; and that's what everyone wants—to be heard and loved throughout a moment.

With trust being so fragile, when it gets broken it is not only unfortunate but consequences are sure to follow. Compare trust to a leg bone that is responsible for bearing the full weight of the body. If the bone is broken, the leg has to be stabilized and reinforced with a cast—perhaps even metal plates or screws. This makes the bone temporarily useless. Not only is mobility not an option, but the other leg takes on extra pressure to compensate, adding to the difficulties. In time the cast can be removed and weight can slowly be added to the hurt leg until it is completely healed. Here is the catch: although mobility is restored it may never heal back to its original integrity and support the load it once did. This would be like trying to hot glue the broken strings on a parachute; sure it may look good and secure on the surface, but when it comes to skydiving, I might take my chances with a golf umbrella.

The same principle works with relationships. If you break your partner's trust, and sometimes heart, by engaging in such things as lying or cheating, or if you make a promise to your spouse or kids and don't keep it, then imagine the clinking and clanking of those trust tokens falling away. They lie there on the ground waiting to be restored, but never to their original place.

Trust in marriages can be reinforced by maintaining a commitment to being honest and dependable. In taking on these traits one can almost predict the outcomes to some of life's challenges.

So consider what trust looks like in the marriage relationship. What areas are you dependable in? If you are falling short somewhere then you must ask whether that is due to lack of ability or just habit. Do I not know how? Or do I need more practice? It helps to take on more responsibility instead of waiting for a cue from an irritated wife. Seize these moments.

When you have a solid trust in your marriage you can walk confidently, knowing that your partner will always be at your side, celebrating the wins and supporting the losses that will surely come.

The Trust Bucket: Declassified

- Trust is fragile, so handle with care

- Know all that you are entrusted with

- Remember the credit/debit system

- Broken trust takes time to heal, so be patient

Chapter 6
SOBERING REALITY

Well folks, here you are. You fell in love, made some big decisions, made a life-long commitment, and now what?

My first sobering moment after marriage was when I realized I had left a stable job, my family, friends and a life that I was carving out for myself in exchange for happiness. Maybe. I found myself with a smoking hot wife and a cold new world away from all things familiar. To say I got homesick is putting it lightly. After the wedding bells stopped ringing in my house I was looking for every excuse to get back home and see everybody. Big mistake! I know now the signal I sent my new bride was that she wasn't the priority she should have been, which made for a rough start. I was reacting to a fear of the unknown.

We went from a whirlwind romance and big party to completing insurance forms and financial planning, all of which hadn't been given a passing thought when I planned to propose. I asked myself questions like, "What do you mean in case I die? I'm handsome, strong and sexually potent . . . those people live forever right?" Remember the earlier chapter where it was noted that women have a more vivid vision of what they want their lives to be like? Well this is it, dudes. Thanks to my wife's proactive decisions, we managed to set up insurance coverage and some investment vehicles right away. These will, hopefully, pay off in our golden years. Most guys will only be looking six months ahead or at the most a year—quite possibly to the next vacation or Christmas holiday.

Women make a lot of decisions based around financial, emotional and physical security. My wife needed to know that if something bad happened, she would have financial support while grieving over her loss and adjusting to a single income and solo life. She also needed to know she could trust me with her feelings and her spiritual needs. Those were some of the major concerns that my wife and most women have when it comes to harvesting the fruit of the union. With that being said as a new husband I was ignorant and unprepared to answer those concerns with any plan or action, and I felt like a scrub for that.

Already from this example you can see where this is going. You may have the question ringing in your minds, what are we supposed to do with each other now? The answer is contingent on where you are in your lives. You may decide you want to play for a while or start planning for family. Either way is cool. Just remember some of the concerns mentioned earlier about taking time to know each other and having experiences together.

The Professional Strategy

The realization that you are actually married and committed to someone can hit hard, like catching sledgehammers with your teeth, particularly when you start to understand all that comes with the rings. Take for example the need to assume the ultimate responsibility for the direction and integrity of your marriage. The role of husband should not be some dead-end job. It should be a professional endeavor. That may sound funny, but think about how successful professionals operate and how they prioritize their time. The pros get their initial training but then go on to take seminars or continued education in their respective fields in order to stay sharp and relevant.

These people need to bypass some of the fun stuff to get things done or fill idle time with something that will advance their skill set. They grind and plant those seeds early, tending them faithfully, so that when it is harvest time they can reap in a way that will be uncommon among their peers. They also network with others who share their goals or with people they aspire to be like.

You can use a similar perspective and make use of these methods in your relationships. Good marriage requires management to make the difference between a magnificent and a miserable life. We should go the way of the new hire who, recognizing the symbolic power and authority of the corner office or big leather chair at the table, sets his eye on them. He decides by so doing he doesn't want to settle for mid-level management, which is a holding pen for people who cover their behinds by throwing people under the bus, killing time until they can retire or vest in the company's 401K. These goals require a vision. Seeking a position without a plan or talents to get there is futile.

The idea of being a professional husband is intriguing, and prompts a new level of thinking. Many wish they'd had these lessons on the front end, but the good news is that all that head-banging drives the point home. It also gives us some wisdom to offer those who are at that point in marriage. With our own torches burning bright, we can light the wick of others and minimize their sobering moments.

Sacrifice Is Essential
A good NFL quarterback can trick a defense by changing plays at the line before snapping the ball. Marriage can work that way as well. If you put that energy into preparing yourself, you have a better chance at defending your end zone. There is a critical concept that helps you at the line of scrimmage, guides you through development of a sound perspective as a teammate and will aid in making tough decisions whether life throws a short pass or the long bomb. The concept is **sacrifice**. I view it as *forfeiting something of high value at a loss for the sake of something broader or greater*. Now, marinate this idea and translate it from dictionary language to heart language.

In a marriage there will continuously be moments where singular wants are in direct conflict with corporate ones. This is the only way to ensure continuity and balance for this living, breathing institution that you are charged with maintaining. There will be instances when both of you disagree on a particular thing. When that happens, negotiations usually take place and wills get tested to see who will break first. Say for example two hundred dollars become available in the budget and a choice has to be made between individual wants and what the household needs. A bigger example would be a parent's education or profession going on hold in order to raise kids or support a spouse who has significant obligations. No matter what angle you take, you will have to give up something. It's important to note that sacrifice is not made with the expectation of later personal gain. The sacrifice is to be done for the maximization of that moment in your union.

You can, in looking back, remember concessions made at one time or another for a greater gain, whether it was skipping a party in high school to study for a big test or not showering in the morning in order to shave ten minutes off your commute to work. (Hey, that's why body spray and baby wipes were invented, right?)

Though the sacrifices we make in our marriages can be vast and in some cases uncomfortable, they all ultimately bear fruit. One means of making sacrifice without completely depleting who you are is to make a "Top 10" list of things you like. Then shave them down to the top three you absolutely love. Don't budge on those. The reason for this is that everyone has a ritual to rejuvenate the spirit. It could range from fishing to playing an instrument. Don't toss out the wrong things. Often the biggest sacrifice is your own selfishness. That cannot make the top three.

As the personal narrative at the beginning of the chapter indicated, a bride should get a rock-solid oath from her groom that he will, without any doubt, protect her body, her feelings and her mind. He will also, with her help and cooperation, lead her through this life with the conviction and purpose of a man on a suicide mission—nothing should stop him from that goal. His bride also needs to know that he has "truly forsaken all others" (Genesis 2:24) KJV and that she is the first thing on his mind. If you are at that point now, it will certainly add a new level of cool to your walk . . . so much that you may need a small band playing your theme song as you glide down the sidewalk!

All in the Family

The next most sobering moment to realizing you've left everything familiar behind is realizing that **her** family is now **your family**. It never dawns on many that a smooth merger of the families may not happen immediately if at all. In most cases much as the families are happy for you finding each other, there are still major differences. The time it takes for families to accept their new son or daughter can vary. Be ready for that. There's a critical aspect that the lovers often overlook: In the family's mind you came into their home and took something of great value away. That can be tough to swallow. Experienced husbands have shared that a man can ease his fiancée's transition into the family by having open and honest dialogue about his feelings, plans and need for their support as he enters this amazing relationship.

A mother may be losing her only son and/or the man of the house if dad wasn't present. Men who have grown up in fatherless homes may miss this dynamic with their mothers or siblings because they are focused on what they are entering and not what they are leaving. Many men are so blindly in love with their wives they don't give much thought to little things like who is going to lift that heavy stuff for mom after I'm gone? Or who is going to help maintain the household in general? It takes many years of holidays with both families to suddenly realize the difference your absence has made and why the idea of seeing your child leave the home can be less than thrilling.

Fathers of girls can say passionately that the day they give another man responsibility for their girls' safety and happiness will be a bittersweet one. They live in a man's perspective. They know how guys operate regarding the opposite sex. The idea of handing your daughter to the wolves can be nauseating. One way of ensuring a soft handoff to your son-in-law is to demonstrate or educate in advance the habits and posture of the kind of man you want her to marry. If you **be it** she will **see it** and ultimately **seek it**.

Most people don't initially have a "jolly" relationship with their in-laws. In the beginning you just learn to tolerate each other at family gatherings. In the middle of this adjustment, there is one investment that leads straight to the gold reserves: stay true to who you are as a person and love your spouse with such a fury that his or her happiness will speak for itself.

When dealing with both your families, be careful to not allow too much access to your relationship. This is *your* marriage, not theirs, and you have to set some boundaries early on before you find your sister- or brother-in-law on a three-way phone call every time you have a fight. Families can be overly protective and often times nosey. It is imperative that both of you have completed the process of emotionally leaving your families and finding refuge in each other. Life has a ton of these for your marriage and your spouse needs to be your first point.

I'll give you an example of a situation and then show how it plays out with and without boundaries. Then decide which river you want to navigate.

Let's say you are having a dispute about the bills and where to allocate the house funds. Things get heated and you are at a bit of an impasse. Up until now, it is just a disagreement about money and you both want a satisfactory resolution.

If there are no boundaries, the wife calls her sister, who happens to be at their parents' house having dinner. She vents over the phone. She may utter something like, "I don't know what we are going to do." After a volcanic spew of emotion and sharing *half the facts* with her sister (usually the facts that back her own perspective), Sister then relays the information to Daddy. Now you have to defend yourself against three people, two of them piling on with blind loyalty to the "victim." Your ability to provide may come into question, which sets you off, and now next Sunday's dinner may be a little awkward. Needless to say the conversation went from A and B to dumping other elements of the alphabet into the mix. Do yourself a favor and put that fence up and manage it with respect and care as it relates to either family's involvement in your affairs.

Now let's examine another course. With this same scenario and boundaries in place, the wife, instead of calling her folks, will resist that temptation and say to herself, "This is our issue and the fix has to come through us."

If you think about it, she has been calling on her family all her life and that's a habit that will take time to break, so you have to deal with your problems yourself. That means you suck it up and lean on each other until an idea comes to mind. At this point there is no outside emotion or ego to manage and it makes for easier problem solving. If there is an impasse, do like a good business would do and bring in an objective specialist, such as a financial advisor.

Time to Work

After the sobering realities of what you've given up and that you've inherited a new family, the third truth to bring you out of the euphoric state is discovering: Marriage doesn't *take* work; it *is* work. Yes, it's cliché, but the fact that being married takes work can't be overstated or over-applied. It is a lifelong commitment that will require everything you currently have and then some more. Everything means exactly that. From your money to your time, it's a direct deposit that should never stop. It seems in this modern era the institution of marriage is being treated like a magazine subscription where you can sign up and get the first six months absolutely free, but when it's time to pay for the other half of the deal, people get disinterested and call in to cancel. This is no different from signing up for a department store credit card just to get 20 percent off a shirt and then canceling after paying off the balance.

When you make that pledge to your partner for better or worse, it is a statement, not a buffet where you can pick and choose which issues to engage. Whether you realize it or not you are signing up for the very best of someone and the very worst. Some situations can be further complicated by unimagined things like an illness or injury that leaves one of you not quite the same. Those moments can expose the depth of your commitment to your loved one when he or she can no longer walk or run or even see.

A Great Recipe

Married life is full of sugary sweet good times and salty bad times, depending on where you left your measuring scoop. A good union is a work in progress. To get your garden of love flourishing takes a lot of sunshine and rain. Here are some truths to help fertilize that sweet corner you are tending and to help avoid the weeds of discomfort:

1. There are no more places to hide
2. Problems are a means to grow closer as a team
3. Conflict is the best way to test your ability to communicate with your spouse
4. Hidden truth thrust into the spotlight creates readiness
5. The problem that's brought up is just a warm-up for the real issue
6. How you recover from the fight is more important than how you started it
7. The differences that exist in your marriage are there to expose you for who you currently are and who you can ultimately be

When a challenge pops up you are faced with engaging or retreating, but to where? You are already at home. You can try to keep your emotions in check and not take the bait, or you can fall for the "head fake," by putting your walls up and commencing to fire back. By keeping calm and not flinching you can withstand the first wave and try to listen carefully to the perceived issue. It helps to repeat it back to better understand. In so doing you quickly realize that this is an opportunity for your spouse to share a hurt and find healing in a safe space. After things level out, you begin to see that there is a deeper problem. By overcoming it, you draw closer mentally and spiritually. By hanging in there and remaining grounded in your stance, you can begin the process of restoration and the trust level kicks up a notch. The benefits of this skill will pay huge dividends throughout life, and you will be emboldened as a husband who feels and knows that his wife can shine the Bat Signal in the air and execute a swift rescue.

Sobering Reality: Declassified

- Men are often not prepared for the onslaught of responsibilities that come with marriage

- Business management problems also work with marriage

- Aim high and seek help in pursuing the goal of a solid marriage

- Sacrifice is essential. Singular wants often conflict with the corporate good

- Her family is now your family, but the bonding takes time

- Practice boundaries regarding family influence on your relationship

- Marriage doesn't take work; it is work

- Face issues head on

Chapter 7

WHERE THE HELL DID MY GIRLFRIEND GO?

If you are amused by the title, then you can probably relate to it on some level. Most newly married men have this conversation, as they watch the women they fell madly in love and lust with morph into someone new and different. This can be a shock because, for the most part, guys are exactly who they are going to be for the duration of the marriage, notwithstanding some wife-inspired changes in habits. It's true that men are simple in what they need and what makes them respond, which is generally whatever is right in front of their faces. Food, sex and silence about sums it up. I'm being facetious. These differences will be addressed later, but it's important to get this common state of the male mind out there and explain why it puzzles them that the girl who used to come to bed naked now enters the bed wrapped in creams, headwear and pajama bottoms with zippers that have a thumb scanner on them.

One guy started out with a girlfriend who was a tiger in the bedroom. When they got in the mix, he didn't have to ask for what he wanted. He would start out in one direction, and from there he would start calling audible plays like Peyton Manning on a two-minute drill to the Oh! Zone. He said the sexual chemistry was off the charts, and naturally it was one of the many things he loved about his then girlfriend. However after the first year the four-alarm fires in the bedroom cooled down to the level of an electric blanket. Yeah it kept his feet warm, but at that level of heat the plastic makes a crackling noise, and you can only use it near a wall plug. Somehow the intensity and variety dwindled away. Before he knew it six months had gone by since he had put on his "naughty cable guy" outfit.

Men need to understand what's happening with their wives that causes them to change focus on that part of the relationship. Here's a major clue: She is thinking about a future that extends past the upcoming weekend, and she wants to make that future a reality. That means things like kids, house, career and maybe even retirement. You will agree that none of those things makes your manhood stiffen when you think about them. Marriage is about more than that.

As discussed earlier, many women have been thinking about getting married since they were little girls, and they have had everything in place except one thing to make it all come together: you. So be prepared for a couple of transformations in your wife from hottie to weekend event coordinator. It is a good thing for husbands that their wives need security in all its forms. It compels them to be concerned for the future. Had this been left up to the men, they would exist like Rambo, thinking, "As long as I got my big-o' survival knife and a poncho for the rain, we will be just fine, honey." Not likely to happen.

Your **girlfriend** used to be cool with coming over to your apartment and snuggling up with you on the couch while your roommate sat awkwardly on the loveseat trying not to pay attention to you making out. Now your **wife** understands that as a couple you need your own space where you can exist and bond. That means a new place, usually a house, where she will begin the process of building her "queendom." There is a universal principle that you will see play out in relationships, and it can drive the harmony in your union— women need security and men need purpose. You've read about this earlier in the book. So as it pertains to a wife wanting a safe and comfortable home where she can start a family, then part of your purpose is to make the resources available for that to be possible. She has not dragged you away from the college football pre-game-preview show to go look at houses or school districts just to piss you off. She is making sure that five years down the road when kids come into play, you are already in a stable neighborhood with a flourishing education system, thus eliminating future stress. Look at it as a down payment on the physical safety of the family and academic opportunity for your children.

Your **girlfriend** used to hang out with you on the weekends and cheer you on at the volcano wing eating contest down at your favorite bar. She also made sure you had plenty of toilet paper and cool wipes when you got home, as Mt. Gluteus would be erupting by the end of the night. Your **wife** on the other hand now shuns that behavior and instead steams all of your meals and initiates her own Spanish inquisition when she finds a crumpled up soda bottle on the floor board of your car. What is the big deal? She never used to have a problem with soda. As a matter of fact, she still holds the record for longest burp by an amateur at the bar mentioned earlier.

She has changed for a good reason. Your wife needs you to be alive and well for as long as possible. History has shown repeatedly that men can be destructive to themselves and others. Your wife will always be concerned about your overall health because the kingdom (or queendom) can't run smoothly without you. So in order to feel confident that her spouse will be there to help facilitate the life you are creating together, she will be all over your ass when it comes to health. If she hears you sneeze and fart at the same time, she will have an appointment made at the doctor's office before you can stop laughing long enough to explain that you are both okay and amused. Statistically wives outlive their husbands. With that little fact staring you in the face, it should be some consolation that she is trying to keep your waistline at a normal size and your arteries flowing swift and smooth like a tube ride at your local water park.

I lost my father to heart disease when I was 12 years old, and my grandparents had to bury their firstborn son when he was 48. I'm now 36, and the thought of checking out early scares the hell out of me when I think about my kids. When it's my turn to answer God's call to come home, I want them to be grown with their own kids. If I've got to trade hot wings and beer for bean sprouts and lemon water, so be it.

None of this means that couples should sit by and let the wild and fun things die in their relationship. You must never let that part of your marriage fizzle out, but a priority shift is essential to make room for more important things like meeting your family's needs now and in the future. These efforts ensure that when it's time for maneuver 14-B from the Kama Sutra manual, then she is all in because business has been taken care of and her sole focus is escorting you to ecstasy and returning you to earth snoozing like a baby.

In closing, imagine two lovers who have left their families to start their own. They find a nice stretch of land to settle. They begin easing into their new and unfamiliar roles. During a quiet moment, the couple sits outside with their backs to each other. The groom is gazing to the west at the sun setting in the distance as he ponders where the hell his girlfriend went. All the while the bride is anxiously awaiting the sunrise to the east wondering when the hell her husband is going to show up.

Where the Hell Did She Go?: Declassified

- Men don't change much; they usually just mellow with time

- Wives have many transitions to face, and men should be aware and supportive of them

- Women think about managing the present to shape the future much sooner than men

- Work together to set a vision for the family

- Marriage takes you beyond boyfriend and girlfriend

- Your new marital title comes with a new set of expectations and responsibilities

- She wants you healthy so you can stick around longer

- Never let your passion for each other fade as your new life begins

Chapter 8
AGGRESSIVE DEBATES, A.K.A. ARGUING

When new couples get home and begin to unwrap the mountain of gifts left by family and friends, hopefully they include his or her mouth guards and sparring gloves for the arguments to come. Perhaps someone may have been thoughtful enough to include the spiritual and emotional equivalent of ninja training for embattled newlyweds. If there is one thing that marriage can assure you of other than an opportunity to forge a love for a lifetime, it is conflict. It would be the rare relationship, real or fictitious, that didn't have some element of conflict. It's the hardest thing to get used to, but also the very thing that matures you in the most necessary of ways. Learning how to aggressively debate with your partner is critical to the long-term health of any marriage. Points are best made to your partner with an understanding of how and when that person is most open to criticism. The natural spousal tendency is to throw up the defensive walls whenever you feel attacked or threatened. That is a reflex that is tough to control, but with time and effort from both partners, you can minimize that knee-jerk response of shutting down and preparing to either fire back or leave the scene.

This whole process is reminiscent of how things can play out at any given job where you have responsibilities and assignments. Accomplishing them determines whether you get paid or not. You can quickly find yourself unemployed for not doing your job. Without corrective action over a period of time, you can ultimately end up jobless or homeless. There is a marriage parallel here. In marriage if you don't perform in your role, you too will ultimately be fired from your job as husband or daddy and possibly end up emotionally homeless under a bridge after a divorce or separation. It's extreme, but it is also way too common.

When emotions start boiling over things can get cloudy quickly and logic can fly out the door like a kid who hears the ice cream truck chiming. If a husband comes home and the first thing he hears coming in through the door is, "Why didn't you _____?" then the immediate reaction will be a counter punch or a pivot out the door. On the flip side, if a wife hears "What's for dinner?" or "I don't have clean underwear?" when she enters the house then she may not only fire back but begin a fifteen-minute speech about all the things that he isn't doing. Definitely you don't want to hear that rant because more than likely you will hear something old brought back up or something she has been sitting on for just the right moment and guess when that is?

There can be a common strategy for bringing up concerns. These work well if you understand that men and women have different windows of opportunity that make them more open to debate. Any man will tell you: the *sneak attack* method is one of the worst. The perfect setting for this is in front of family or in a public space where everyone can hear. There is no worse time to have a situation escalate than in front of others, particularly children, because the only thing that follows that flare-up is embarrassment and vengeance. If you are a practitioner of this method, you will always lose in the long run and suffer collateral damage.

There are some strategies that work, not only in personal relationships but at work as well. Here is a list of times that aren't on the best seller list for dumping issues on men. Women certainly have their own lists. So please don't try to raise issues, when men are:

- Trying to eat
- Trying to go to sleep
- Watching a football game
- Watching a favorite show on TV

- Being pulled over by police
- In pursuit of sex
- Recently home from work

Here are some times that are best for bringing up concerns to guys:

- After a meal
- At least ten minutes after waking up from a nap

- When it is *crystal clear* that his sports team is going to win the game

- After ensuring him that the program you have interrupted is in fact being recorded for later viewing

- Post-romantic climax and a sandwich
- When the officer releases you with a warning

It should be obvious that these are all periods of time when a man is trying to relax or unwind. You will read more about the importance of a man being able to relax in Chapter 14, "The Hall of Don't Bother Me." Winding down is when a man is able to transform his mind from battling the day to nurturing his domestic responsibilities. All guys would love to come home and tune out for an hour, but the feasibility of that may vary based on household. Anyone who has been married for several years knows that there is always "something" that needs to be handled by Super Dad or Ultra Spouse. Sometimes that very thought can give a dude pause before he comes home and turns that knob. (This is not a negation of women's need for down time, but this book is aimed at understanding how men think and how their way of thinking, when properly understood, can shine in a marriage.)

I used to have a family member who would come home from work and take a twenty-minute nap in the driveway before he would go inside. I thought it was weird then, but after early morning start times and two young kids, I perfectly understand that he was transitioning. As a matter of fact, I have thought of taking it one step further and parking my car under an overpass and pretending I was dead. If the Highway Patrol pulled up, I would at least get an extra forty-five minutes of sleep before the medical examiner showed up, at which point I would miraculously wake up, thank Jesus and speed away waving to the officers.

Never overestimate the complexity of the male mind. In reality it generally doesn't handle well more than one thing at a time. If the subject of his attention is not right in front of him or on the border of his peripheral vision with flashing lights and noise, it might as well be on the other side of the universe. Within this lies a strength and a weakness. The strength lies in men being able to focus on a single task all the way to completion. A man can focus on quality, making sure all the tires in his wife's car have sufficient tire pressure or that all the bolts on the kids' new play gym have been tightened to a point that you would need Superman, the Incredible Hulk and Zeus in order to loosen them.

The weakness comes in the form of a man who just got his butt handed to him by his boss. He walks in the front door of his home, not yet having fully processed the matter, and is assaulted from all angles about something that *hasn't been done* or *needs to be done.* He may not be able to switch gears fast enough to guard against a knee–jerk reaction. Subsequently he dives into a fight-or-flight mindset. What's important here is both men and women knowing their own weaknesses and those of their partners, then bearing those in mind when communicating a tough issue. That's the best recipe for only having to handle it once.

It's Okay to Not Like Him or Her Today

This statement gives validity to the flux of emotions in marriage. There are days when you have looked at your loved one and thought, "Today, I would love to just push him out into morning traffic, but I won't because that notion includes jail time, and I have burned up all my sick days at work."

You all have had these moments when you were upset with your spouses and found yourselves momentarily thinking some crazy stuff. You need to know that is okay to have that feeling well up at times. It means you give a damn about being happy with your spouse. What is *not okay* is taking that emotion, creating an unbreakable bubble around yourself and walking around the home ignoring your spouse. It's a common defense. But, in the end, whether it was a few hours or even a week, how did it help solve your problem? It flat out didn't. The silent treatment will not cure what ails you; it only buys more time for one person to get even angrier and the other one to hope the other one "gets over it."

Often, men will leave the house and go have a brew or get something to eat, instead of sticking in the fight and resolving it. When a man leaves the house and doesn't come home for hours or even the next morning, he has achieved only one thing: more trouble. The last thing you need is a woman sitting at home filling in the blanks about what may be going on in your absence. A man could have driven around the block and slept in the car by a neighbor's house. Seems harmless to him. Not so much, because all the wife knows is that you two had a fight; and you got pissed off, storming out the house to do God knows what. Here is where it gets tragic. In your absence, the wife's mind is running a million miles an hour. She is imagining the script to a story about what you *might be* doing: everything from getting drunk to spending the rent money on a cheap hooker and getting into a shootout with the police. Sounds funny, but without you there to quash that process, it might as well have happened. So, again, how does this help? The toughest lesson to learn in an argument is to walk closer to the fire, rather than away from it.

In one case of fighting in the extreme, the wife got so hot that she didn't speak to her husband for a week. It takes a lot of energy to purposely not talk—not engage someone with whom you share space—and it can be spiritually draining. After the couple made peace the woman exclaimed that the emotional toll on her wasn't worth the prize that her pride had bought. Please think on these things as you have arguments. Before you act, think about what the next step might be. It bears reiterating: If the strategy is to walk away from the problem, then you have only pushed the "pause" button. The situation *will* be waiting for you to get back; with 20 percent interest.

How Can We Resolve Conflict?
Conflict is resolved every day. Millions of times. The best way to handle it in the home is like a customer service representative dealing with an irate patron who seems to want something unreasonable. You've been in line at a retail location and seen this play out. The customer gets fired up and the clerk

either reacts to the venom and gets on the same level, which usually gets the employee in trouble, or stays unaffected by the yelling and the insults. Upset people who lash out are in fact inviting you into their emotional tornado. When you choose not to take the bait then the winds die down, the debris falls to the ground and you can focus on the real issue. This strategy is sound, and it works in a multitude of scenarios. On the surface it may seem like you don't care. If your lover charges you with indifference, you simply reply, "Baby, I care enough to hear everything you have to say, so I can figure out how to help us get back to happy." It is an indirect way of saying, "Get it all out of your system so we can talk like two adults." From here, you have saved your union from the silent treatment and also given your lover a hint that she doesn't have to set the house on fire just to be heard.

The need for great communication in a relationship can't be overstated. If good communication is a well paved highway allowing for swift travel back and forth, then poor communication is an old foot trail through the Appalachian Mountains. The consequences of poor communication and where it can lead is encapsulated in the following analogy drawn up by one husband who felt he'd been there. At most traffic lights or highway ramps in cities across the country, he noted, you are likely to see a panhandler or a vagrant, asking for money. Most motorists have mastered the art of "ignoring what's in front of them." They act like they are on the phone or look the other way. They may look straight ahead, behind the anonymity of sunglasses, as this person approaches. For a moment they may contemplate what this guy's poor life choices were that led him to sleeping under a bridge in a hopeless cycle of not catching a break. For this person you see the immediate consequences of his ordeal and yet mostly people turn away. After all three little dollars aren't going to get him off the street and change his life. Or will they?

In any work environment you, alongside others, have to cooperate to complete your task in a much larger process. And the big motivator is: if you don't cooperate, there are immediate consequences, like write-ups and termination. For most there is some level of fear associated with losing a job because of the need to provide the family's wants and needs. If there is a problem at work you address it in order to maintain the job.

When you are married and in a committed relationship but fail to be transparent and informative with each other, then you err on a couple of levels. First if there are problems and you don't let your partner know, then she can't react or come to the rescue. Second you abandon a fundamental trust to emotionally provide for the other. You can't simply get offended by something said or done by a loved one and remain silent while this noisy soundtrack of how you were wronged is blasting inside your mind. All the while, your spouse is oblivious to what is going on. Being emotionally supportive means you have to spit it out and put it up for debate. As in a workplace setting, you have a duty to report any wrongdoing, and so it should go in your marriage. In a work setting, you have a code of behavior in place to prevent unwanted behavior and so should it be in your marriage. In a work setting you get rewarded for over performance, and so shall it be in your marriage.

By way of illustration, let's say a husband has an ongoing beef with his lady and he fails to resolve it with her. He continues to exist in the home as if there is no issue, and adopts the philosophy that, "She's just crazy!" This lingers on and now her frustration turns to apathy as she assumes, "Hey! My feelings and thoughts aren't of any value to him." At this point, as in a lot of work settings, a problem has been reported and nothing done. The next step is to take matters into your own hands and do what you feel is right in your own eyes . . . Uh oh!

It's plausible to say that emotional and spiritual distance likely swells between the two and now the hunt begins for someone or something that will "value me or take interest." The offended party begins masquerading after hours at bars or chat rooms to find this acceptance, all the while keeping up appearances at home. Remember, the spouse knows there is trouble, but doesn't want to deal with it. After months of secretly shopping her "resume" around, she is offered a new gig with better pay and benefits for her children. She has now reached a point of peace about leaving because she has found new emotional security elsewhere. Now comes the letter of resignation, which completely catches her husband by surprise. After all, *this came out of nowhere*, and *I had no idea you were* this *unhappy*. The separation is made and now ex-husband wanders about completely relieved of his spousal duties but saddled with failure and loneliness. Don't worry though. He can take his mind off his misery by projecting it on those around him, until they too run out of the patience needed to deal with his crap. The now ex-husband and ex-friend rises months later and finds himself awakening with a big yawn, scratching his unshaven face. He looks up to see the sun but can't because the bridge is in the way.

Some folks say that it is healthy to fight, and it probably is on some level. Veteran spouses realize that the big blowups and knock-down, drag-out fights aren't necessary once a relationship has gotten to the point where you can be hurt and offended but still somewhat civil about how to tackle a tough issue. Experience teaches a husband to be ready for anything and be surprised by nothing. This means that you should be ready on any given day to deal with any emotional outburst, a request for backup or some type of call to arms in an emergency. Men should be prepared to be beaten down by the world and still have enough left in them to come home and find one more skirmish left to deal with. Sometimes you just have to find another gear to shift to. This ability to shift should come from a place of preparing your minds to leave one environment and its challenges and enter another with its own set of challenges. You can't develop it any other way except being in the middle of a feud and trying to get to that place where emotion is present but no longer in control.

There is a saying that nobody can hurt you as much as the one you love; that statement ranks up there with the best. The funny thing about being in love and surrendering yourself to it is that it leaves you completely exposed and yet it is the only posture where love can have its most potent effect.

In spite of your attempts to contain the fire, when you fight and argue with those you love, you can lose yourself in the moment and say things you don't mean, or commit some egregious act that plunges you deeper into turmoil. The challenge in these moments is to summon a new level of courage. From this summoning comes the courage to be brave enough to not lose control or abandon your spouse because it is getting hot in the kitchen. If patience is not part of your process when arguing, then you are asking for more anger and fewer solutions to the problem. When two very different people share a life then there will surely be conflict. But once you are at peace with knowing conflicts will come and you are equipped to manage problems through to a reasonable ending, you can stand tall in the weeds. Now you can be present and available to your partner, so you can lead her into the open fields of resolution and restoration and celebrate your emancipation from turmoil's persuasion. Praise the Lord!

In closing, I want to share a personal story about a practice suggested by my then girlfriend now wife as part of a new holiday tradition. It has helped keep us in tune with each other's thoughts and desires throughout our years together as we mature as spouses. We created the "State of Our Union" letters. These letters are written separately in the days leading up to New Year's Eve. As part of the overall celebration we read them aloud to each other. The letters can be many things from a declaration of how much you love the other all the way down to an itemized list of things that pissed you off this year. There is always an agreement that the other one has the floor until they are completely finished at which point questions or comments can be given. The purpose of this is to make sure that nothing is left unsaid between us and it also serves as an archive to look back on in the years to come. We often laugh at how selfish and trivial we were in the beginning. With this practice we always understand where we stand, whether it be favorably or not, and the letters gave voice to unmentioned concerns and allowed for a chance to address them. Our hopes are to give those letters to our daughters when they get married so they can see the evolution of their parents love for each other.

Aggressive Debates: Declassified

- Disagreements come with any relationship
- Learn **how** and **when** to talk to your partner

- The truth stings for a moment but the hangover from lies or silence lingers

- Strive to be emotionally available to your partner

- Communication will either float your boat or sink it, depending on how it happens

- Everybody deserves to be heard and most folks will

- Find someone to listen at any cost

- Deal with the little fires now and not the raging inferno later

- During arguments, learn to run toward your partner and not away

- Always know the state of your union

Chapter 9
HUSBAND OR DO BOY

Today people are extremely busy and overscheduled. This would include spouses. Many husbands will find themselves rushing to do it all for the family, but at some point the question arises: Am I her husband or just her "do boy"? If this struck a nerve with you then take a moment to pause and center yourself. The response a number of husbands offered regarding their association with the word, "do-boy," was part of the impetus that drove this book. When asked for the first five things that came to mind when they hear the word, they offered the following list: *Weak. Errand Boy. Crony. Chauffeur. Servant. Puppet. Secretary.* And lastly, *Bi@#h*. You don't want a translation.

These come as no surprise, as you've heard many of them before. Generally, a "do boy" is someone who is subservient, unable to demonstrate intelligence, someone without a backbone and a gopher. I'm not aware of many dudes that would sign up for this role. If you have been married more than a couple of years then you have had your bout with this, or maybe you still are. Feeling like this is freaking horrible. As one husband who felt like his wife's employee said, "You feel like you are on an assembly line working your tail off in a place with no clocks and no break area; you are just sitting there looking up at the track, waiting on the next thing to come flying through the chute." Men find this arrangement confusing and infuriating at the same time.

Most of them have no problems working hard, but they do need to know why they are doing something and, more importantly, that their efforts are *appreciated*. This is particularly important to recognize if your partner is asking you to do things that she wouldn't do. That just makes you feel like a fool. You may be talking to yourself saying things like, "Well, I want her to be happy," but that is only a temporary fix.

So what do we do about it? The work won't go away, nor should it, because you are in the life-building process, but the help comes from a shift in attitude and perspective. This can happen when the shot caller takes an honest inventory of what is critical to the household and what is just errands. This level of delegation can overwhelm the "doer" and liberate the "thinker." It is careless to overburden our spouses without regards to other things they may need or want to do.

Diagnosis

In attempting to navigate these waters, the first thing to understand, as you have read, is that your wife has had a master plan for your lives together since before she met you. She was just waiting for you to fill in that blank and then "happily ever after" was supposed to follow. With this in mind, you might be advised to expect the barrage of "honey-do" lists. However you currently handle those will help you figure out if you suffer from the plague of being a do boy. To overcome this, put yourself on the *"planning committee"* with your wife, and actually get a look at the projects to-be. Most new husbands are bamboozled into thinking that after picking out those drapes on Saturday afternoon they will be home in time for the game, but not so fast! You have no clue what the overall window treatment needs, and therefore when she sees the sale on curtain rods at another store and hangs a left, you start boiling. Most dudes either explode or begin the silent pout routine, where they walk around with their jaws set tight. Gentlemen, if you get involved in this project from the start, then you can assist with time management and not spend several hours getting re-routed. The other benefit to this is that she will appreciate the time and support even though she knows you couldn't care less about whether you get new drapes.

And then there is the self-imposed Jedi mind trick. It starts out with you evolving into your natural role as a leader, and by this I mean taking the initiative to find out what the desires and plans are and then discussing them with your wife to formulate a plan, as mentioned. You see, what applies to drapes, applies to everything from hunting for a dog and fixing up the yard to getting the kids signed up for everything mom wants them to be in. You are written into the contract.

Keeping Perspective

It's important to get involved for another reason: Wives sometimes forget all the balls they have thrown up in the air for you to juggle and someone has to raise their hand and say, "Hey Baby, I know you want to sign Junior up for this class, but it starts at 4:00 p.m. and it will run over into karate, swimming, art, Boy Scouts, piano, chess and archery classes on Tuesday." That overall view of what is going on with the family's activities is crucial to keeping your lives in perspective. The family will need a lazy Sunday every now and again. When you take the initiative to try to co-manage tasks and appointments, what you will see is your wife taking notice of you having a new impact on the family.

In these modern times women have moved into the work force and assumed roles that were traditionally held by men—a positive thing—but it did create a void in the household when Mama is no longer present to stabilize the household before Daddy gets home. Now both parents are working and the question will lie out there on the horizon: who is responsible for maintaining the house? The answer should be obvious: you both are, as a single unit. What couples need to discover is the beauty and efficiency of having a battle buddy to combat life's demands and limitations. Since you both made the decisions and entered the conflict together, you move with confidence because your partner has your back and vice versa.

There are other ways of doing this, which you may try with varied success (including getting downright pissed off with each other) but working as co-planners and co-executors seems to work.

With the first method many try, the wife comes home from work and does it all while the husband kicks his feet up, feeling satisfied that he has brought home the bacon for the day. He spends the next hour and a half watching

Sports Center and grunting about how tired he is, while the wife begins steaming under the surface. Things that boil eventually boil over.

The second way involves making the "chore list," like you when you were a child. "Okay, Baby, you got the kitchen and the bedroom, and I'll take the living room and the garage." Eventually, there ends up being a task that needs to be done more frequently and then it will seem like one of you is working your butt off more than the other. She may say, "Big Daddy! How do you have time to play golf, hike, learn a second language and feed the poor three times a week?" To which he may reply, "Well, Babycakes, when we divided the list up, I took the gutters, oil changes, air filters and the fish tank," which are not daily tasks, all by design. This too usually ends up in frustration.

The third option was the charmer for us, and the idea came to me in a flash. I put on my leadership hat and pitched the strategy to her: "We both live in this house; we share the rewards and the upkeep alike, so why don't we adopt the policy that no matter where the mess or problem is, if you can handle it right then and there then do it." Neither one of us carried on looking for a reward or pat on the back. The change was swift. My wife began to see less dirty laundry when she got home, and I noticed an absence of bowls in the sink with dried oatmeal in them, waiting for me to chisel it off in the afternoon when I came in. What we also found was that Saturday clean-up time got shorter and shorter, allowing us to spend more time together. That's what we all wanted: to come home from work and school and enjoy each other's company, instead of being a bunch of worker bees inefficiently maintaining the hive.

As I began to recover from my "do-boy-itis," I began to understand how our relationship morphed and grew as a result of me stepping up and extending myself.

Recovery in Action

Guys would agree that wives love to make decisions and to have an element of control in most household affairs. That is natural and normal, as long as there isn't a monopoly on influence (that works both ways, by the way). There are instances, however, when the husband is the better fit to make the call. We live in the realm of action and in that realm there are consequences for all decisions that we make. Men's lives have been an endless stream of, "Let's see what happens if I do *this!*" The good side of that is that men are more prepared for the unexpected and experience has taught that a little pre-appraisal goes a long way. Sometimes our wives are not prepared for the fallout of a decision gone south. For example, women and girls have a license to break down at any time and no one judges, but let a dude start losing it, then suddenly the invites to poker night get fewer and fewer.

So let's say Honeybuns is in love with the idea of having a fire and water element in the backyard. You guys make the arrangement and spend a couple weekends at the hardware store picking out crap to go around it and in it. The buzz is strong right now because the "plan" is coming together nicely. You get everything up and running and have that party outside that she envisioned when she saw it in the magazine three weeks prior. After receiving the high fives from the other wives, she is on top of the world. However, after a few months the gas bill from the torch gets higher and the imported koi fish from Japan are belly up because you decided that you shouldn't be the only one feeding the damn things. Then reality sets in that maybe this "backyard spectacle" should have stayed in the magazine.

So, go back to the start and think about what you could do differently. Instead of going along, you object and respectfully decline to participate because you foresee the outcomes. She may not like you for a couple of days, but she can't argue with solid logic and truth. The good news is you dodged an extension of your duties, a hike in utilities and a lot of dead fish. Pressing it any further just seems like a "princess" moment.

When you turn away from the dark, cold and unrewarding ways of "do-boy-dom," and walk tall in the warm light of husbandry, you will see your wife begin to willingly release her grip on certain things and default to your judgment, or at least take your feedback seriously. This sounds good right—having your wife take a step back and allow you to maneuver in your natural role? This can only happen when you have achieved one critical thing: her *trust*. Earlier you learned that your wife needs to feel secure, and that can only happen after you have shown and proven that you can handle whatever area of life she is releasing to you and be effective at it. If you can pull this off, then you will usher in a new level of harmony and fulfillment into your relationship.

His Way vs. Her Way

On the flip side of this opportunity lies a terrible but rewarding challenge for your wives. The reward lies just on the other side of an acknowledgment of a particular truth: **When he does it, it is not going to look the same as when she does it**. Women need to get comfortable with this thought. Men say countlessly that wives are in their husbands' butts every time they extend themselves because they may not be "doing it right." It may surprise some women that there are multiple ways of doing any given task, and you can end up with a similar result. A perfect example is bath time for kids. You may run some warm water and check the temperature with a fifty-dollar thermometer you purchased from the baby store and then measure out a specific amount of hypo-allergenic, gluten-free, non-dye and non-tree-nut based baby shampoo. From there you may even softly caress sweet baby's soft skin with a cloth made from discarded angel wings, all the while singing a sweet, sweet melody. Husband on the other hand may just shoot some Palmolive in the tub and stir the water with the baby while he is beat boxing his favorite rap song. Either way, you end up with a clean baby that you can see your reflection on.

If he doesn't know how to do something such as taking care of the baby or which one of your blouses can actually be washed and not dry cleaned, then show him what you do or what the desired result should be. I guarantee that nothing makes your man's tail wag more than finding a solution to a problem. He will shout to the heavens, "Hear-ye, hear-ye; I no longer know *jack* about washing the delicate clothing. And all my undershirts remained bright white because I quit throwing red hand towels in with them." Besides, he knows if he was a red hand towel, he wouldn't want to be all alone, and would certainly prefer warm water over cold. You can do that if you are with like colors. In addition to this new knowledge, he may also figure out a way to shave five minutes off his wife's personal best time. Three cheers for MAN power!

It takes a lot of effort to run a household. When your spouse sees you having an impact in the areas that you are able, the energy in your home will transform. As mentioned, most men don't have a problem with working or having to find another gear in order to get something done, but they do have a problem not receiving something in return for their efforts. Usually a sandwich or some sex will settle any outstanding charges. However, that can't always be the reward (not to discredit the wonders of sex and sandwiches). Most guys need to figure out how to be satisfied with just getting the day's work done and wives need to show appreciation and respect for the effort of these Mighty Titans they married.

Men are wired for action and so they should be active in all aspects of their lives, not just their professional ones. A man who is working "for free," in his mind, will certainly have the attitude of a toothless squirrel at a peanut factory, so it is important that his wife helps him understand the value of what she is asking of him and demonstrate appreciation as deeply and as often as possible.

Husband or Do Boy: Declassified

- No successful person has ever done it all by themselves. We all need help and a break

- Men are willing to carry the load for the family, but will soon stop if they feel like "do boys"

- Get more involved in matters around the home in order to find efficiencies and to have a voice

- Don't expect a man to remember more than three things at a time

- Women work off a master plan. Help keep it realistic

- Rather than make chore lists, base who does what on what needs doing and who is available

- He is your partner not your employee and should be given all the respect due to him

- Women need to understand it is okay to have different ways of doing things

Chapter 10
SEX AND ROMANCE

Note to the reader: If you skipped straight to this chapter then please return to your place in line.

It may seem there isn't much left to be said about sex and romance. Rather than rehash the familiar, you will explore the utility and value of sex and romance in a relationship. While portrayal of sex and the dialogue surrounding it is usually focused on sensual gratification, it can also maintain the spirits and heal relations. Sex is much more in-your-face compared to twenty-five years ago (damn, that sounded old). On a daily basis, you are bombarded with sexual images and suggestions at every turn. You can't look at TV or listen to radio without hearing a lustful outburst or seeing some well-sculpted vixen, wearing a napkin and dental floss, selling ketchup. Who would have connected the two? You can't even wait in that long line at the grocery store without boobs or six-pack abs yelling at you from the magazine rack, while the old lady in front of you buys $3.50 of cat food and pays with nickels. So with this level of stimulus in your face every day, it makes perfect sense why a lot of people, guys in particular, are overly obsessed with having sex.

A study was highlighted in an article in *Psychology Today* (September 20, 2010 issue) stating that 54 percent of men surveyed thought about sex several times a day. When they looked at the rest of the pie, the fewest thoughts about sex were still a couple times a week. It also cited that women's drives were slower, particularly after entering relationships. Sexuality is a natural drive that can't be shut off, but like all drives, you can choose not to be ruled by it. There will certainly be moments in marriage that need to take priority over you getting your rocks off. An example might be a one-sided bedside conversation about the kids or bills that need to be paid and Big Daddy listening with a zombie-like stare on his face mumbling, "Yeah, yeah, that's real *nice*, baby. Now how about some action?" He should be able to exercise enough self-control to hold the line until he has paid attention to and settled the matters at hand—and then from there you two can get tangled up like a string of Christmas lights! (It is to be noted that this book did recommend earlier that the business end of the marriage not be addressed at certain times when a man is unwinding, including when he is going to bed.)

The Boom in the Bedroom
There is nothing in this world like making love to a person with whom you have a deep spiritual and emotional connection. The energy that is transferred, and absorbed, can take away all your cares. It can also heal a wounded heart. Yep, sex has more uses than duct tape.

Sex is like most things in life; it's all about what you bring into it. You can have a casual encounter after a night of partying and get that tingle you've been searching for all night. Of course, it is completely void of emotion or connection—just a primal clash of private parts. On the other hand, you can align with someone on an emotional and spiritual level and get fulfillment before any actual physical action begins. These moments can be spine rattling.

That spine rattle is different from the accountability-free tingle from casual sex.

Changes in Sex
One of the things most men discover is that sex after marriage changes. A lot. Men often come into marriage immature and unable to fathom why things are changing. You may be puzzled about why you were so spontaneous and reckless about sex as boyfriend and girlfriend, but now as husband and wife there can be times when you may have to make an appointment for some

bargain-barrel loving. You may be shaking your heads on this one because, like many men, you've been there or *are* there.

The change in sex provides an interesting challenge when you are under the assumption that her body belongs to you and vice versa, which should be true; however, it doesn't always play out that way. It doesn't have to be that way. In fact the sex should get better and better as you learn each other on many different levels. You can't compete on the long-term with short-term factors. When you are dating, there are days that go by without seeing each other, which can generate excitement. That changes when you are living together. It could be that the excitement wears off and you have to make time to get that fire going again. The challenge here is taking something familiar and revitalizing it. Compare it to a thunderstorm that starts out with a cold front and a warm front dancing around each other on a daily basis until things line up just right and then the thunder and lightning explode on the scene.

Let's look at the main reason that sex changes after marriage. It's pretty simple. Your LIFE changes after you get married. Most of you have had job pressures, relocated to another city or maybe even a child has come into play. These three things alone can usher in a ton of pressure and obligations that can knock intimacy down a rung or two on the priority list. Think about all the things you are responsible for on a daily basis. Men generally feel because they got up and worked all day, took the trash out and lifted that heavy stuff that the wife couldn't handle their day is rubber stamped and should be worthy of some sort of access to sexual gratification. Yep, you come home and plop down on the couch and exhale. If you do this, then your list of responsibilities is probably relatively short, and there may be the faint sound of a spouse's teeth grinding in the distance.

Compare this scenario with that of the modern-day working mom, who has done the same thing, but also has to coordinate the family's evening routine of dinner, bath and housekeeping. She, too, is looking for that time to exhale from her day and it's usually at this moment when she is about to do this that Big Daddy comes strutting in with that look on his face signaling that it may be time for his "medicine."

Clearing Out the Queue

You have possibly found yourself in the common posture where you are poised to pounce on your beloved like a lion on an antelope, when your gestures are derailed with, "I'm not in the mood." This phrase can be perplexing if you don't understand the language of women. You think, "what do you mean, not in the mood?' I brushed my teeth and everything." It takes very, very little to set us off. However, for a woman, it really is about mood and mindset. You see, a woman's mind can be like your smartphone when you get a text message and don't acknowledge it; the device will keep chirping away until you check that message. Now, how in the hell does this relate to sex? Easy. If she is getting those alerts about things such as the bills, kids, condition of the house, a family member, work, a friend's drama or even the argument you guys had last week that didn't get resolved because you walked off, then those messages are standing in the way of her "mood."

Your mission as a husband is to check off those alerts as they come in, to the best of your ability. This way, you can clear out the inbox and leave one alert blinking that says, "Husband needs some loving."

If you want to prime your wife for intimacy, then think of helping out more around the house or consider random acts of kindness as one version of foreplay. Of course, you have the traditional romantic gestures that still work, but they don't work in a vacuum.

It's essential for couples to understand the importance of each other's sex drive because after all, after you said "I do," where else are you supposed to get it handled? Think about that for moment. If you behave like sex and romance is that Disney vacation you intended on taking but haven't because things are busy right now, then you are letting each other down.

Married folks need to keep pre-marital and pre-parental romance alive. Think of it like this: your spouse is the love you started out with, and after careers and kids have had their season, it will be the love you are left with. Be mindful of this. Don't let your romance go the way of that old car sitting in the backyard that has been neglected to the point that you don't even feel like dealing with it—flat tires and rusted quarter panels promising even worse under the hood.

Experimentation

In figuring out what gets those spark plugs firing, you might be surprised. One man made an astounding discovery as it related to pursuing sex with his wife. Like most guys, he felt like roses and dim lights would put her in the mood. That seems to be a baseline for most guys, probably because it worked when you were dating. What he discovered was light years away from wine and roses.

On his off days, he picked up a little bit around the house and especially vacuumed the carpets. What he didn't know and found out was that the sight of those 45-degree angle lines on the floor going to and fro in a fan-like pattern made her body tingle on the spot. He was floored by the response. After you quit laughing, here's the take-away: it really did come down to a man being able to take her mind away from her work or burdens long enough for his desires, or even hers, to register on the screen. So please note that you may be able to get just as much action from making up the bed and putting your underwear in the hamper as you would with a lobster dinner and roses. Also, apparently, vacuuming has some aphrodisiac-like properties.

The Healing

Marvin Gaye sings a song called, "Sexual Healing," where the lyrics paint a picture of a man needing to release all that burdens him. He finds that in the lap of the one he loves. This can be true for everyone, man and woman alike. There is a healing aspect of sex. When you are there for your spouse in a time of need, you can transform yourself into a vessel in which they can release themselves and get centered again. Indeed sex can sometimes cure what ails you.

There is no closer level that you can get on with someone than through sexual intimacy. When you're being intimate with someone you love, you can be completely naked with them spiritually and emotionally, with no judgment and no reservations. If you have never come home from a hard day and just taken your spouse into your arms and got buck wild until your cares just melted off you then give it a shot; go home and heal the one who loves you.

This being said, new husbands need to understand that everything can't lead to sex. Intimacy is less physical and more emotional, particularly for your wife. The emotional component of this is typically a new arena for guys, so gals need to patiently help their spouses understand what they need. Husbands may not appreciate or be cognizant of this aspect of a woman's makeup. Since it is uncharted territory, his tendency will probably be to turn a blind eye or shy away from it. For example your wife may have had a hell of a day and was almost in tears at one point and all she wants to do is come home and curl up under your manly arms and just *be*—*no* groping, no dirty talk, just a safe place and a kind word letting her know she is at home. Spouses will both need this safe place to retreat to. The best practice is to use the golden rule and respect the need of the moment. If you don't want an intimate moment ruined by a random request to hang Christmas lights or look at carpet swatches, then equate that same feeling with desperately needing a hug and being offered something less emotional instead.

As you learn your wife's emotions, please take the time to be attentive to them and nourish them the same way you do your fantasy football account. If you aren't getting much productivity out of the current strategy, then analyze it and change it. But don't go on Facebook or Twitter and update everybody about your sex life. That part of your life is sacred.

Make Love to the Mind
Your wife needs to feel safe and secure in all things so through intimacy you can communicate to her that, emotionally, you "see" her. Her feelings are safe with you. She will need to feel like a priority in your life. We all share that need. Guys tend to fix things and bring finality to any situation. It will be a little counter intuitive for you to maintain, rather than seek an *end* to a feeling.

For example, your wife might be having a bad day because of her asshole boss and wanting to release that to you. A typical guy response might include a shift from his wife's emotions onto wondering what time this punk takes his lunch break. A better choice, of course, would be to steadfastly allow the full range of her feelings to flow. At some point, you can expect her to gaze up at you and deliver a kiss for being in her corner. Should your emotional availability stir up something inside her, then you can put the red light bulb in and let the reckoning begin.

Navigating these emotional waters takes patience and understanding. There is a certain closeness that can be had by just sharing space on the couch or laying in the bed, curled up, and letting each other know what is going on. Fellas may think spooning and not thinking about having sex is like giving you $1,000 at the hardware store and expecting you to just *look*, but it can be done. There's a theme in this book about not being "ruled by your Johnson."

Regularly, couples overlook talking about sex in an intelligent capacity, as opposed to the general bragging about what's getting ready to go down when you get home. Underlying much of what goes on is the lack of knowing each other that is characteristic of new relationships. As you become more comfortable together, you should be able to communicate to your loved one exactly what you like and how you like it, in order to set yourselves up for a more fulfilling sex life. Why wouldn't you want to know what he or she likes? You could certainly save some time by not executing some elaborate maneuver that she doesn't like. Instead, you could put your energy into rubbing her body with a feather if she is delicate, or you could throw her into a full nelson and shout, "Who's the master?" if she prefers things a little bit more physically aggressive. Either way, a successful and healthy sex life is one where you know for sure what makes the other one ignite into flames.

Now, one of the first questions to rise from this is: "What if I like this and my partner doesn't?" Great question, because there is a high probability, with the level of pre-marital sex in our culture and the infiltration of pornography into our lives, there will be differences and preferences.

Fantasy vs. Reality
The adult porn industry is in the business of fantasy. Plain and simple. The actors are just that, actors. Real-life couples cannot maintain the level of eroticism. The characters seen in adult films probably aren't working 50 hours every week and raising children. It's important that we not allow too much of the fantasy to bleed over into our reality. Consumption of this material can set some unrealistic expectations for spouses.

For example, a man who looks at adult material with 6-foot blonde bombshells in it is probably setting his five-foot two-inch brunette wife up for failure as it pertains to him being satisfied. On the flipside, a woman who is reading too many romance novels about a tall shirtless Norwegian riding a horse along the beach will probably be see her short, overweight husband sputtering along in the yard on his mower as a buzzkill.

A young man acknowledged there were unresolved issues in a prior relationship that went on for about a year. That sounded normal enough until he ranted on about all the things he was doing to win her over from paying bills to babysitting. He stressed that he felt like he was being taken advantage of, so he broke it off. Here's the clincher: he ended the complaining with the statement, "And out of that whole time we were together she only performed X-rated gestures two times." That immediately prompted the question: exactly how many times was she "supposed" to do this for you? As if women are universally bound to a specific level of eroticism. If they are on board with it, then so be it, but if not, then you need to get past that and *leave* it because of all the other wonderful things in your relationship. If you're being honest, none of you wanted to marry the fast chic. She may be fun, wild and at your command, but you may have to watch her around your buddies. She's not permanent material. So why would you try to turn the woman you chose to marry into her?

Men have blurred the lines between what they see on TV and hear in popular music to the point that they think all women are on board with pimping themselves. It's simply not true. And when you are partnering for life, why would you want it to be? What you are looking for is a partner in your life who will support and challenge you in all areas. So how do you bridge what you desire in fantasy and what you seek in purpose? First comes respect, then the discipline to stand by it. If you love someone enough, if that person isn't comfortable with something, now or ever, then you have to be all right with it. That's not a free pass to not experiment or try new stuff with your spouse, but there are limits. If your wife asks you to come to bed naked, wearing only a backpack and some roller skates, you're probably going to pass . . . quickly! And she's probably going to get over it quickly. You might want to ask her to just hold you for a little while instead. Never mind what she might want in that backpack. Whatever your appetites may include, just make sure you give your spouse the chance to say, "Yes" or "Hell no."

In conclusion, married sex has gotten a bad rap in recent times because it is portrayed as two miserable people simply going through the motions. In some cases that is true, but equally true is that this part of your relationship can be explosive and spine-rattling, if you know how to set the stage and which buttons to push. In a union, the only limits that should be placed are the ones you've agreed upon, because, hey, it's your life not your neighbor's. However, your neighbors may end up wanting your sex life once they hear what sounds like a lion and a Tasmanian Devil going at it on the other side of the fence.

Sex and Romance: Declassified

- Sex is awesome and necessary in a marriage

- It can be therapeutic and bring healing

- Help her settle her thoughts

- Have fun and experiment, but respect each other's preferences

- Understand the divide between fantasy and reality

- Too much adult imagery can damage your drive for your spouse because there is a digital intruder

- Through intimacy, you make love to the mind, and from there the body follows

Chapter II

OUR MONEY

When I got married it was with the understanding that from day one, our two incomes would become singular. From this singular pot we would distribute our hard-earned dollars toward all our liabilities as well as our wants. We had many discussions about finances during our dating and we discovered that while we had very different spending habits, our aim was generally pointed in the same direction. The question that would arise was, "How fast do we get there?" The answer often depended on who was willing to sacrifice what. We both agreed that debt was bad. We wanted to get rid of it in hopes to have an experience with money unknown to many – being free of the dreaded "minimum payment due." We also strived to get on the same page in understanding not what our money could **buy** for us but what it could **do** for us. I was admittedly slowest to get on board with financial discipline because of my past habits with money. I would be that guy that would get bills in the mail and figure out how to make several tiny payments, leaving me with enough to go have a tiny bit of fun. I saw no use in delaying gratification for the promise of **big fun** later. I was like a very stingy and misguided bank teller in my dealings with my own finances. I felt clever as I short-changed the envelopes "One for you, and three for me."

In retrospect, we were very fortunate in bridging the habits of Spender Man vs. Saver Woman. Financial discipline has aided in keeping us close together because all money matters are made together. This alleviated us from the fate of households with one shot caller and a spectator waiting to boo and throw popcorn at the first miscalculation. Partnership here is key. We started this journey together and we will continue to work toward determining our own financial future.

For the Love of Money

The Bible says that the love of money is the root of all evil; and it is highly evident in our culture what the love of money had brought us—usually greed and excess. Gone is the idea of money as a means of exchange for goods and services. In the present day it is an *identity* or an *address*. How many reminders do you have on a daily basis that you don't have enough money? Interestingly, the guy driving a beat-down bucket who makes $30,000 a year, is asking himself the same question as the guy in the Mercedes whose annual income is $130,000. That question? How can I get more? The lie that money can make you happy and cure all that pains you is pervasive in our society. And it's simply not true. Money is an inanimate object that has power because we give our power to it. Yes, you got that right: we give **our** power to **it**. It's an act of the will.

Money can't love you; it can't make you feel secure; and it can't make you okay with who you are. Nor can money buy you true peace and harmony. What money *can* buy you is tons of things. Such as a marching band to follow you while playing your theme song and a blimp hovering overhead with two old guys narrating your every move. The fireworks will be furious and frequent at every pose you take and every snappy comment you make can become viral in moments. It can also summon lots of people who will distract you from your lack of peace and harmony. It is very rare to see a broke guy with a bunch of posh friends and beautiful women hanging off of him, unless it's some sort of outreach project to raise awareness about some poor sap who can't get a break.

Public Enemy No. 1

Why address money and our attitude toward it at this point? Unfortunately, a leading cause of failed marriages is the inability to discuss money and how it will be managed. If you want to see where a person's heart lies and survey what they truly value in life, just tinker with his money a little bit and see what happens. You probably got your first view of differences in how you value, spend and save money when you were planning the wedding. The collision between what you want and what you can afford sends ripples into fantasy land. It is very easy for couples to lose sight of their budgetary limits in the midst of planning such a big ceremony. It is far too common for new couples to rack up thousands of dollars in credit-card debt in order to make that special day come true. What also comes true is the reality that you have started your lives together with a big boulder to drag around with you until manage to chip away at it. It's safe to say that your first dream vacation may have to wait until next year. Problems related to money can usher in a tidal wave of stress into a relationship that can sometimes lead to extreme frustration and even divorce. How many divorces you know about resulted from someone's lifestyle not being maintained or being downgraded? Things like job loss or company restructuring can hit a happy home from out of nowhere and now all of a sudden your wife's champion, provider and love of her life is now a bum. You sense she can't stand the sight of you, much less be honest in bed. The hurdles that arise as a result of a lack of money are too expansive to run through individually, but commonly couples take a serious deathblow to their harmony when the checks are not clearing the bank.

How can a love so strong have the rug pulled out from it over something like money? It's the old cliché of "no romance without finance." What does that say about a culture when people hold love hostage for a ransom payment? Money is a necessity. You can't run a household without it, but avoid the mistake of taking on the *identity* of money in your relationships. It can lead to the destruction of a true love, which should transcend the fleeting condition of your bank account. Indeed, money is not only essential but having it is fun.

It is exciting to be able to travel and do stuff that you couldn't otherwise do on a tight budget making ends meet, but it certainly shouldn't be the chief motivation of a relationship.

Who's the Master?
Money only wields as much power in a relationship as we allow. That is more evident today with a swing in the trend from dad making all the money to mama regularly bringing home the bulk of the income. That starts to raise the question: Who has the final say on matters in the relationship? Short answer is you both do. It's often telling of a relationship when the husband and wife have separate accounts for paying the bills. This situation screams out that there might be a gap in the level of unity between the two. We are in this thing together aren't we? If I eat, then you eat and vice versa? Not combining finances is like going to a party with a friend, who wants to drive his own car, "Just in case I want to leave early." Kind of selfish; kind of uncommitted, is it not? You leave when everybody else leaves, that's basic teammate stuff. Withholding tactics are about control on some level. If on one hand you have one partner who is careless with money and spends every dime, pouting until next payday, while on the other hand you have one who saved money, that partner is *safe* and now *in control*. Instead of the spender learning restraint and the saver learning to let go a bit, the saver either dictates the next moves or continues enjoying accessibility to money until payday comes. There is nothing in this game plan that would suggest these people are on the same page; in fact it may actually suggest the contrary. If there is a difference in philosophy between them, it is a gap that has to be bridged, immediately. Money should simply be a tool or a means of facilitating the family's objectives, not an indicator of status or authority. Interestingly enough, money habits may only be the vehicle or the delivery system for some deeper issues.

An example could be behavior that is based on a sense of entitlement, much like the teenage girl who puts on an Oscar-worthy crying scene in the lobby when her folks tell her the newest phone is too expensive. The reverse of this might look like an individual who didn't have much money growing up and feels like you have to hold on to every little bit you get. You may picture a character from a movie who sits in a cave filled with gold, silver, experiencing the accompanying paranoia that someone is out to steal it. This person may have a nice savings built up, but also hasn't had a wardrobe update or taken a vacation in five years.

We also can't leave out the adrenaline junkie who makes purchases purely of out the thrill of acquisition. There could be a hunter's instincts at play here as this junkie pauses before entering the mall to put on retail camouflage and war paint. From here our spending addict stalks the clearance rack with patience, being careful to check the XXL section to see if someone short on cash tried to hide a medium in there before running to the ATM. After the purchase is made a wave of delight sweeps over our big spender and it lasts all the way home, only to be filled with self-reproach and the need to turn around to take it back. Hopefully the return policy isn't exchange only.

When it comes to paying the bills, there can be a lot of stress and frustration around financial obligations—especially when you are starting out. In most cases, there is one person who is the go-to person when it comes to balancing checkbooks. In most cases, it is mama because her predisposition toward security makes her desirous of designating the funds. It is particularly important to remember that keeping the books is a task, not a dictatorship. Yes, it is true that the household can't afford to be sixty bucks short on the light bill because Dad stood in line last night to get the newest edition of John Madden football. The reverse of this is also true; Mom shouldn't come home with new heels if the daycare tuition hasn't been paid. No matter who takes the lead, it is paramount that the other person have some current knowledge and proficiency with the finances should one of you get sick or be out of town on the week the bills get paid. That dynamic in itself can cause stress if you feel like you are the only one who can do this one thing and everyone else doesn't care or is unable. So if you are not the primary bill payer in the house, show your other half some love and carve out time at least once a month to figure out where the money is going and why. The additional benefit is, of course, that you may have a better idea that improves either your spending or your financing practices.

What Can Green Do for You?
As you already know, vision is critical in most aspects of family life. Finances are no exception. If there is no vision for the family as to the direction where you are heading or how fast to paddle then you are on a homemade raft drifting

in the ocean. Your vision should be the compass by which you steer your family toward the goal. This is critical. Too many people pour their hearts and souls into their jobs week after week and then waste their hard-earned money on frivolous things that have no long-term value. Examples are endless, but they often share a common motivation. Take for instance, looking "large and in charge," which, incidentally, does not move your family forward. Driving a car that cost 25 percent of your monthly income doesn't move your family forward; living in the "right neighborhood" with a mortgage that doesn't allow you to furnish it or go on vacation doesn't move the family forward; and indulging in an excessive lifestyle that drains your resources doesn't move the family forward. In fact, these can drain your coffers to the point where you make no progress toward things like paying off your current house, funding the kids' college fund or zeroing out student loans. It creates a self-induced bondage that you can't get past. Most of you have heard the cliché, "Work hard; play hard," and it has an element of truth to it. However it cannot exist without its counterpart, "Work smart; live well." We were born to be more than customers and account numbers. If you want to have money and not let money have you, then press "9" to hear this message in English.

You read at the start of this book that this realm profits from fear and pain. That in turn drives many of your decisions. You have to break the fear of not being the sharpest dressed every single day, when you spend $150 on books and trips to a museum. Rather than buy the latest basketball shoe or spend $300 on the next soon-to-be-obsolete smartphone after rebate open your child a bank account. For the guy who has a family and plays golf or goes drinking every week but hasn't bought anything for his wife in six months, be it flowers, dinner or her favorite wine, then there is an opportunity waiting there for you. Who knows, you may even get some nonobligatory loving.

Hopefully, you and your spouse will take time to set a vision for what your family needs —leaving out your wants—and plot a course, including boundaries, for how you behave with the family's money. You may find in the midst of this that other issues come up that aren't a result of money. Often money is used as a coping mechanism for something else, and that deserves a separate conversation.

Some number crunching in the good times department could help you with realignment:

- Eighteen holes of golf and a cart: $50

- Wings and three rounds of drinks for four: $75

- New PlayStation game: $60

- Poker night (depending on level of luck): $50 to $200

- Adult entertainment $100 (holds you for thirty minutes unless "Sunshine" gets on stage and starts twisting and wiggling, then it increases dramatically): One trillion dollars,

You get the point. You are looking at hundreds of dollars a month in random activities for popular entertainment in a culture where, according to a survey from HowtoSaveMoney.com (March 1, 2012), Americans spend about 94 percent of their income. This only leaves six percent to be tucked away somewhere. Americans experiencing an emergency that required $5,000 in cash couldn't pay it. Now look back at the party items listed and realize that it doesn't include most of the ladies' leisure activities. Most people party, spend or subscribe their way to broke, every month. Then when life happens, they go into debt or depression trying to deal with it.

This book is not intended to demoralize or discourage anyone from having a good time; rather, it is calling for an increase in financial literacy so people can build a more stable foundation on which they can party better for a longer period in their life.

Absolutely nobody likes to be broke. If you have realistic plans for your money, and benchmarks to help you stay on track, then you can set your children up for a better life— perhaps better than you had.

Our Money: Declassified

- Husband and wife get on the same page with money

- Bringing in the bigger paycheck doesn't mean more budget authority

- Have money, but don't let money have you

- Ensure your financial foundation will support the weight you will put on it

- The family's needs come before **your** wants

Chapter 12
FATHERHOOD

This chapter holds a special place in my heart because it addresses one of life's most precious gifts, and that is the relationship with our children. They are both the one thing you would give up your kingdoms for and, on some days, feel like trading for a pizza and an hour of silence. You can't prepare fully for marriage or parenthood because the variables differ exponentially from one couple to the next. Much is learned on the job. Nothing will highlight this more than your own journey from a self-centered person to forsaking all the things you once did on your own time.

I have two small girls and can speak on this phase in detail; however, there are principles in play when children are little that gain importance as they get older. Children bring with them unlimited potential, but also vast responsibility, and I hope to bring that to light by the chapter's end.

New Daddy

The birth of a first child is an awesome event. Your reactions to it are unfathomable in advance. Depending on how strong a stomach one has; the sight of seeing your child delivered from out of your partners' bodies can be either traumatizing or incredibly beautiful.

When my kids were born, it gave me a renewed appreciation for what my wife had been going through nine months prior and was currently going through, being stretched out on a hospital bed, surrounded by masked strangers and her jerk husband who facilitated this process in the first place. Yep, I didn't imagine this moment many nights ago when I was feeding her sliced mango, exchanging back massages and singing old, school love songs. I was looking for a little action-packed fun and, now, I find myself holding this little organism that came with no directions. Now the real fun starts.

After the buzz of the family's and friends' excitement wears off, there can be periods of fear and anxiety. The reality has hit that you are now responsible for caring for this child. It usually sets in when you come home and your old routine has to now be immediately replaced by your new one. No more two-hour naps or hanging with the crew past midnight. You are now at the beck and call of a little person who has **one thousand** different and specific needs and uses only **one** sound to alert you to all of them. The sound of my daughter crying was perplexing because I didn't know what in the world she wanted. Was she hungry? Did she have a dirty diaper? No, turns out she wanted to scoot over three-eighths of an inch farther down on my chest. Turns out that is what all the ruckus was about after I had changed diapers and wasted a perfectly good bottle of premium breast milk. Ah, and here comes another whole new world: Breast Milk. I capitalized it because it deserves that and so much more. If a wife decides to nurse, then that's great for Dad and Baby; but not so much for Mom—at least in the R & R department. The site of a new mother saddled with a backpack with tubes and pumps attached to her can conjure up images of an astronaut or some super villain from the planet Lacton, who is searching other worlds for alternative dairy sources. In reality, one of the most precious and awe-inspiring moments for me was watching my wife with our baby, in that moment where they gaze at each other and introduce themselves physically, spiritually and emotionally. Witnessing this was one of many glimpses into what my wife had been going through and also what was lying ahead.

There came a point where I began to start feeding my daughter and trying to put her to sleep at night, and that's when I came across a few intimate truths that I and other new fathers may have missed out on: the deep level of peace and serenity I felt with her on my chest while I was rocking in the chair. As a side note, I highly recommend a gliding chair with a leg rest for those long nights ahead.

Past Asleep

Anyone who has had kids can profess from the mountaintops about the challenges of those first six months with a new child in the house. There is one particular challenge that can and will ruin any marital bliss you and your wife may have; it goes by the name of *sleep deprivation*. If this was a movie, there would be thunder and lightning in the background, with a shadowy figure standing atop a volcano laughing and mocking. Yes, my friends, the days of sleeping through the night will be a fond memory. Hell one might as well throw the clocks in the trash, because there is no need for an alarm and leaving the house on time isn't going to happen for a while. You might as well make peace with the fact that both of you have more bags under your eyes then the lost and found at a border crossing known for drug trafficking.

Supporting Role

Not since the Civil War have we seen family turn on each other in the way that sleep deprivation invokes. Mike, here, can you share an example? Lots of them! The preferred technique of husbands is either the North American opossum or West Texas armadillo pose. This response kicks in when the child begins to cry at 2:00 a.m., after being attended to just forty-five minutes prior. Big Daddy initiates a corpse-like position and pretends not to hear anything. This stance is immune to a wife's nudges, sighs, sarcasm and even water in the face; however, the mere mention of possibly losing access to the wife's "goodies" has been known to wake the dead. Now get your behind up and grab the baby!

In the fight against sleep deprivation the only way to defeat it is through forging an alliance with one's spouse and developing a buddy system, such as dad changing the diapers and then mom nursing. If formula is in play, you can try fixing three or four bottles in advance and taking a tag-team approach. The idea behind this is that no one person gets more sleep than the other and the animosity is kept to a minimum. Teamwork is the only surefire way of managing the challenges that infants and newborns present. Everything from establishing a sleep schedule to dealing with the "sniffles," will call on parents' deepest levels of patience and resolve to care for the child and still find a new gear in order to go to work the next day and function enough to avoid getting fired.

No Judgment

We find out exactly how much patience we have—and how unaware we are of what it takes to embarrass us – when we take young kids out to a restaurant. In order to get the adventure started, one is sure to ask the hostess for a booth or table that will accommodate the three pieces of carry-on luggage that were dragged in behind baby, containing: diapers, wipes, formula, baby food, four changes of clothes, changing pad, two bottles of medicine they aren't old enough to take yet, and who could forget the dirty diaper that was changed at a long traffic light and didn't get thrown away.

After setting up base camp, we're ready to order food, which will be timed to arrive just as the little pumpkin is waking up from that seven-minute nap that prompted us to think we would have time eat. This can be a critical moment. We know they are programmed to wake up with either a full diaper or an empty stomach and, as we learned earlier, they alert us with an ambulance-like wailing that is sure to get the attention of the other patrons. Parents will immediately be able to distinguish who has kids and who doesn't by the empathetic grins or the scowls turned their way; but no need for fear, because super dad is prepared, through training, to have a room-temperature bottle on his hip next to his smartphone, just in case this moment arose. Anyone who has been caught out in public without a bottle premixed and ready to drink knows the searing heat of panic and despair as the parents try to console the baby and find a source of purified artesian water that simply has to be processed through reverse osmosis and blessed by a shaman! Whew! That was close. Now that our precious angel has been attended to then everyone can eat in peace. Cold steak anyone?

I'm making fun of a moment that all new parents face, but in all seriousness, there is no better joy as a parent than being prepared and ready to spring into action when your child needs something. There is no price on the trust that builds between husband and wife through these events. It also serves to develop some thick skin against people who look at kids as if they are cell phones with obnoxious ringtones their parents refuse to turn off. You just learn to hang in there.

I have learned so many little lessons in my short time as a father and I stand ready to learn more as new scenarios arise, but I stand confident in being able to manage them. I've learned a few truths, the ultimate of which is that as a father I am responsible for my children, who came into this world knowing absolutely nothing about it and need me to guide and protect them as they grow. Whenever I find myself getting frustrated with my kids when they are "flicking" lights on and off or opening a random cabinet door for the 20th time, I try to picture myself being dropped into the middle of a city in China. I've never been there, and I certainly don't speak the language. I picture how foolish I would look trying to communicate with people or trying figure out what a sign says. Those thoughts ground me as I take a deep breath and just watch my 2-year-old spin all of the toilet paper off the last roll in the house.

Quality Time
Another lesson I have learned is about "undivided" attention. If I'm being honest, I can't think of anything on which I actually sit and completely focus. I mention this because all children I have played with or witnessed appear to live in the moment. That being said, I should be able to be "present" in those moments with them. While walking down a sidewalk on my way to the car, I may not be struck by the difference in a red pickup truck and a blue, two-door sports car, but for them it's something fascinating and worthy of an explanation if they inquire.

Kids have more questions than one of those debit card machines at your local retailer: Why should I have to answer seven pages of surveys to buy a stick of gum? The more of my children's questions I answer, the more complex the next set of questions. This is, however, how they understand the world, and if we want them to have it better than we did as kids, then we had better make sure they have more of their curiosity engaged at an earlier time and deeper level than we did.

I like to look at the process as if the whole world is just on the other side of a tall brick wall and every question I answer is like a brick being stacked in the form of stairs. When they get to the top and survey for themselves, children will be gazing from a solid footing. Hopefully, from this vantage point, they will decide what lessons learned have value and which ones don't. The saving grace is that they have them at all. Parents, take a bow!

Unconditional Love

I learned one other lesson from my wife, who showed me what love can add to your life when it's genuine and plentiful: never ever underestimate the power of an "I love you." Children, both big and small, go through life seeking love from someone or something. When children hear us tell them that we love them, and when they can see it in our eyes, it will fill them with joy and bond us together in a deeper, more meaningful way. A parent's love will make a child feel secure and confident. They know you will be a refuge they can run to should they misbehave or have failures in life, and that you will always be a safe place where they can get their courage up to get back out there and try it again.

We have all either been the person or have seen the person who strived to gain acceptance or validation from people who did not value us and who certainly did not reciprocate the affection. These affection-craving people, however ugly or beautiful, wander desperately in an invisible, desert wasteland seeking something genuine and fulfilling. We, as parents, can spare our children this sorrow-filled journey by letting them know every day how much we love them and that we are committed to the protection and nurturing of their hearts and dreams. There are few feelings greater than having our child run up to us, randomly give us a hug, and shout, "I love you mommy and daddy," as they squeeze our neck or leg with all their might.

Oddly enough this stuff works for adults as well, although they don't usually squeeze your leg due to Human Resources pesky little "rules."

We should also assist our kids in dealing with their fears and teach them how to distinguish the difference between their unique fears and danger. Fear can keep you from trying things that are challenging or difficult, while danger will likely decide how you address the challenge. Usually, boys excel at this.

In essence, fatherhood is a lot like being a high end hotel concierge with a bazooka and a broom strapped to his back. He is expected to know the answers to all things including the best places to eat and the shortcuts to get there. The bazooka comes into play when something goes "bump" in the night and he is ready to "bump back." Finally the broom is for sweeping up the shattered remains of everyone's poor choices, including his own.

Fatherhood: Declassified

- Fatherhood is one of life's greatest experiences

- Be mindful of the sacrifices that you will have to make

- Sleep deprivation is the real enemy, not your partner. Develop a team approach to lessen the impact

- Children will test your patience

- You will develop thick skin when it comes to those who judge you because your children are being children

- Start your parenting with the end in mind

- Take time to make time for them. They are only this size once

- Undivided attention is priceless

- Your unwavering love and support will give them the wings they need to fly

Chapter 13
KIDS, AND THEN THERE WERE THREE

After a few years of life with kids, you find yourself asking two questions: "What the hell was I thinking by reproducing?" Then, "How have I made it without them?" Seriously. What rational adult would knowingly sign up for the chaos and depletion of patience that kids bring into your life? When you bought your last brand new vehicle and looked around at the interior, did you picture it missing a floor mat or even having an assortment of crumbs and half-eaten candy resting firmly in that spot between the driver's seat and console where no human hands can reach? And don't forget the faint smell of three different fast-food restaurants lingering in the interior. You probably didn't ask for the princess stickers plastered on the inside of the door, either. Yes, the inside of a parent's car looks like someone picked up Disneyland and shook it up like a snow globe, then set it back down. Wait for it; here comes the point: You never know how kids will change your life, but you do know that they will. People complain about the negative impact kids have had in marriages. What did they think was going to happen?

Welcome to Earth
Children come to us knowing absolutely nothing about this new alien world we have been living in all of our lives. Their new home is foreign along with

the languages and customs. They will spend the rest of their lives trying to learn their environment and find their place in it. The duty of mothers and fathers is to provide all the useful knowledge their children will need to become independent.

It would be awesome if kids were born with the understanding of basic physics principals such as gravity, centrifugal force and momentum. This knowledge could possibly eliminate falls from beds, stains on walls from swinging a spoonful of baby food over their heads and maybe even bumps on heads from taking a corner too fast in dress socks. Since they don't know this stuff we have to be there to fill in the gaps.

Moms and Dads would be well served by reminding themselves every single day that kids don't know what we have already learned and that's why it's important to live in their moments with them and pour into them what is useful. If you don't, be assured that someone else will.

Whenever you bring children into the picture, whether they are babies or teenagers from another relationship, then you have been charged with an oath to be there for them and lead them. You may not have a document stating this, but it is written in the eyes and hearts of those young people in need of your love and guidance.

Your union with your wife should provide an atmosphere where kids can develop into who they will ultimately be. They have a lot of learning ahead. They will need to know everything, from how to deal with conflict to learning the confidence to chase their dreams. If that isn't the case in your home for whatever reason, ask yourself, "What am I doing in my home to make this happen?" Quick hint: the answer won't be found on ESPN or HGTV. Sports Center offers dudes a lot of great action and entertainment with tons of highlights, however none of the broadcast end like this. "Whoa! What a game! The defending champs have been destroyed; now let's turn back to the guys in the studio and find out how to keep a wonderful kid from ruining a great marriage." You also won't see interior designers laying out different ways to **spruce up** your marriage through lighting, pop colors and adding some accent pieces from reclaimed wood. Why? Because you have to D.I.Y.

Sticking Together

One of the toughest adjustments in raising kids is making peace with the fact that a wedge, albeit positive, has been driven between you and your partner. The days of having a drink after work or pumping iron at the gym for three hours are all but gone. The kids take center stage. If this sounds depressing, then you are not alone in thinking that.

In the past, I found myself feeling frustrated and anxious from missing **my time** alone or just curling up with my wife and watching TV. According to my math, there are 168 hours in a week; take out sleep and work and see what it is left. There's not much time to get in all the things a husband and wife need to do to stay fresh. It becomes very easy to lose sight of each other in the midst of having kids. My wife and I have learned the power of the almighty date night. Some of these have been spent on actual dates, and some have been spent just trying to get some uninterrupted sleep.

Any parent will tell you that keeping your spouse on the radar is hard because of the constant interruptions from kids. As with your professional life, just because it's hard doesn't mean it can't be done, and it is certainly no excuse not to try. Just think about any big victory or lesson you experienced: it usually came with some struggle. It is never good when spouses go days without actually talking to each other about anything substantive, particularly the current state of the union. I've found that a random, "Hey baby are we good?" Can provide some comfort to my wife that I'm thinking about her. It also provides advance notice of danger ahead. Either way, this simple gesture can pay huge dividends on a regular basis.

The fallout from not keeping your spouse as a priority can be crazy. Men openly confess they felt like a second-class citizen after kids came along because of the intensive care and attention young babies require. One man says he was demoted from Husband, Lover and Friend to the Diaper-Dude, Formula-Man and Mr. Midnight Medicine Fetcher. These titles reflect the requirements of new fathers, however silly they may sound.

Another man stated that when wives become mothers they can completely lose focus of their wifely duties. This is NOT an indictment on mothers. It is his opinion and it is related to his experiences. He found himself steadily moved out of the position of Center of the Universe over to Planet Who Gives a Damn. This gentleman wasn't allowed to help out with his own child for some reason. How utterly, ridiculous. Men want to care for their infants as much as moms do, even if they don't know how yet. The desire is there. Again, remember that sometimes guys shy away from things they fear. So this man did what a lot of guys do, which is take the path of least resistance. He found other things to do. Seems harmless right? In this case, he found other things to do until his children went off to college. At that point, his wife woke up out of some daze with a now empty nest and wanted to be wifely again. Only problem is that her husband had become accustomed to being left alone until he was absolutely needed and so that's what he wanted to keep happening—being left alone.

This story can hit close to home, because it is a glimpse into a future that awaits countless other husbands if they don't act early in their relationships. The warning here is that you shouldn't allow yourself to be marginalized because of your kids. Even if you have to set up every date night and arrange all babysitting for the evening, it is vital to keeping mommy and daddy connected. There will be plenty of days and nights when you either think there is no time to fit it in, but for the sake of your *original love*, please try.

Modeling the Future
The payoff for keeping an element of romance while raising children is not only that both parents still feel "wanted and desired" no matter how frequent or seldom the opportunities arise to act on it, but you will be directly displaying to your children how a man and woman love each other.

Please don't underestimate how these positive images manifest themselves in your own children's romantic lives when they become of age. We must remember that we are their point of reference for everything from how we walk to how we handle problems whether it be good bad or indifferent. They are like little tape recorders with no tiny red light to let you know the power is on.

On an aside, the adrenaline rush of "sneaking off to get primal" in the laundry room for a few minutes can be exhilarating. Laundry rooms work because mama bear isn't going all the way to the other side of the house away from her little slumbering cub to get her groove on.

Another solid piece of advice when it comes to balancing parenting and getting some action: you may want to set up some booby traps like trip wires, lasers, trap doors or dig a moat in front of your bedroom door. Hopefully, this will aid in early detection of little feet stealing quietly towards your door in hopes of finding out the source of the noise keeping them awake.

There is nothing worse than being close to arrival and your spouse coming to a dead stop (no pun intended) and uttering, "Was that the kids?" That's like watching your football team get ready to kick a field goal in overtime for the win and then the power goes out.

This may seem like a fantasy to working parents who are making it happen every single day for their families. The struggles of being tied into a daily routine seem to soak up all hours of the day from school drop-offs to band and soccer practices. You feel like you spend the day on auto-pilot, just going through the motions until it's time to land. You may pause long enough to remember you haven't rubbed your spouse's back or had yours rubbed in a long time. To remedy this, try switching that mindless TV show you watch for your spouse's attention, and see what happens.

We tried this in our home. We did not watch *any* TV for an entire week. I was amazed at how much more time we had to talk, laugh and make each other relax and feel good, however that needed to be achieved. So if you want another challenge besides raising little people, try having some non-digital nights with the one you love and deserve.

Kids: Declassified

- Mom and Dad need to be in a good place in order to create a love-filled environment

- No matter a child's origin, his or her needs never change and that is your love

- Exercise patience, patience and more patience

- Remember they haven't learned what you already know

- Mom and Dad can't stop being husband and wife

- There little camera is always rolling, so be mindful of what they see and hear

Chapter 14

THE HALL OF "DON'T BOTHER ME"

Every superhero turns to a secret lair or compound after fighting injustice abroad. Batman has his cave, Superman his Fortress of Solitude and even the Smurfs have their own little mushrooms where they can retreat after an adventure: nobody messes with them during commercials. The average guy needs his own retreat space, or at least access to one. Men have a rough time knowing where to go for peace and stillness after a long day of working a job and fighting off all the things the world throws at them.

So where can a mighty man go to get relief? If you are married and/or have kids, then the answer is probably: Nowhere. This can be a problem. After taking major hits at work, you really only want one thing and that is to grab the remote, elevate your feet, and softly exhale with a *premium curse word* and relax. Men, mostly, choose to plop down in front of a TV and have their minds numbed for about an hour in High Definition. The majority of men enjoy a healthy dose of silence, at some point, to clear their minds and decompress from the day. It is a sacred time for a man, a transitory place where he can tell his boss to go to hell and his family to wait about twenty minutes before you bombard him with requests. All this tough talk happens in his mind, naturally. Truth is, most guys are into their family's desires and jump right in to participate in whatever is going on. There are times when this can seem like trying to parallel park a jumbo jet in a fast-food drive thru. The challenge comes when the Husband Express comes barreling in off the highway, it will need enough space to slow down, turn around and change out passengers. He is dropping off work and picking up family, so please allow a little slice of time to change gears and refocus.

Give Me a Minute
It needs to be understood, at this point, that we are not endorsing a man coming home and welding his butt to the couch with an "out of order" sign on his chest. This is more about the male wiring. Men just seem to need seclusion and recharging like women crave social interaction. Unfortunately they either need them at the same time, or their obligations mean neither is able to get what they need. This is where, in a mature relationship, you carve out those times for each other—working it out according to your particular circumstances.

While the term "man cave" has become a popular word in our culture, it not only suggests a dimly lit and cool place, but an environment that it is secluded and exclusive. Before bonus rooms and man caves, men would hang out in the garage or an old shed in the backyard. Those who couldn't find a solitary moment to themselves on their own property would frequent a local pub or watering hole where other guys were seeking a retreat from authority and obligations.

This may seem a dismal picture, but to the contrary, it illustrates a need men have that may be unknown to their wives. If knowledge is power, then the women and children in these men's lives have just got hold of the world's largest lithium battery. If this need is recognized and addressed on some level, it will definitely contribute to the overall health and energy of the home. The notion that "If Mama isn't happy, then nobody is happy," shouldn't be exclusive to just Mom. A woman's work is neither painless nor stress-free. Women should be celebrated more often for their contributions to making men's lives so livable. If there is a mutual interest in Dad having a baseline of joy in his life, then there is no end of the earth to which a man won't run to for his wife and kids. Not only will a well-rested and well-appreciated husband tackle whatever you throw at him, he may even exercise some initiative and handle stuff before you even think about it. That's just how we are wired, always looking for the next thing to brag about.

Nothing on the Radar

Whether our families believe it or not, there are times when men are thinking about absolutely "nothing;" seriously, there is not a single blip on the radar. It's almost like a dormant state of mind where you are waiting on stimulus, such as noise or motion from a kid's shadow trying to sneak into the room while you are napping, or the obnoxious inquiry being yelled from across the house by your wife, "What are you doing?" Men across the nation know exactly what this is like. Women cannot always identify, but they can try to understand.

Polishing the Armor

So the "man cave," the "decompression chamber," the "executive suite," the "hole" — whatever you want to call it—is a place of sanctuary where a man can feel whole in a masculine sense. Picture a dude coming in from battling the world. He returns to the castle gates to be warmly greeted by his adoring family, who shout his cheers and praise his bravery. His eldest son takes the reins of his horse and leads it to the stable, while his fair maiden tosses a perfume-laden handkerchief indicating that after he showers it is "about to go down." He acknowledges her gesture with an affirmative wink and an appreciative head nod. Make sure this is happening in slow motion, by the way. From there he makes his way through the kitchen. Here, he tears the drumstick off of a freshly roasted turkey, prepared by the earlier-mentioned maiden. He picks up his pace as he draws near to the one place he desires most and then an abrupt pause, for he is now at the doors of the Hall of "Don't Bother Me." He kneels and pays homage before entering this hallowed hall. As he steps in, shuts the door behind him and hovers over his favorite chair, his legs collapse, and he falls back into his **sweet spot**. Ahhhhhh! A grand sigh erupts from his lungs as he tosses his sword on the floor and spends the next hour in a dark room scratching his feet and farting. You may laugh, but it is happening in bonus rooms and master bathrooms all over America.

MICHAEL R WARREN

Hall of "Don't Bother Me": Declassified

- Every man needs some space or time to himself to decompress and change gears

- A well-rested and appreciated husband will break through brick walls with a spatula to provide for his family

- Men need to know that they are being effective in the home

- That blank stare on his face while watching TV is just that; no need to overthink this

- Men take a lot from the world and their family so this maintenance in necessary

- The "Hall" is not a force field protecting from responsibility

Chapter 15

CREATING ACCOUNTABILITY

If ever there was an opportunity to reference the "dangling carrot" dynamic, it could certainly be applied to creating accountability in your relationship. In all relationships and agreements there have to be expectations set and consequences for not fulfilling your end of the deal. In a generic sense, the carrot will be the vision of an existence with our partners that is rooted in trust and certainty. The good thing about this image, as it applies to marriage, is that you do get to consume the carrot in the end. You're not just a cart horse who stupidly follows the elusive carrot until he drops dead in his traces.

There are plenty of reasons for mutual accountability in marriage, but the main one is to protect your relationship from negative influences and poor judgment. Every day, moment by moment, we make numerous choices. Sometimes people don't think about how the fruit of their decisions affects their marriage or how they appear to others. There should never be a question whether a husband or spouse is *accessible when needed*. Being accountable also redirects behavioral patterns and helps to shape mindsets when it comes to maintaining your love life. So if we find ourselves in the company of a dude who invites us to an underground fight club and doesn't answer his wife's calls because he told her he was volunteering at an animal shelter at 10:00 p.m. on a Wednesday, we will probably want to second guess tagging along.

Set Yourself up for Success

Accountability is particularly important when it comes to both spouses' outside relationships. Men freely admit to situations they have put themselves in with co-workers that conveyed a different perception of them than how they would like to be viewed. Take "George," who is married, works in an office setting and whose assignments require him to work with "Jane," who is single. The interactions these two have on a daily basis have to be managed carefully, because it is only human nature to become comfortable with a person if you spend enough time together. Initially, in such a situation, there could be no attraction but that might change if conversations stray from "work" to "personal" issues. Your thoughts on the quarterly review could easily shift to reviewing hind-quarters if you're not careful.

These things shouldn't continue over into phone calls or emails being responded to in another room away from George's family. I can't tell you how many arguments that I have come across that involved someone giving up the password to their phone; unless you work for the C.I.A. or have nuclear launch codes in your phone then you should be at ease leaving your phone on the table while you use the bathroom.

The occasional lunchtime outings with Jane can and will be viewed by others as something they may or may not be. There will be a perception that something is brewing. As a married person, it's important to think about this because you always need to ask yourself this one critical question: "Would I do this if my wife were standing here?" That question ushers in accountability and strategic thinking about your choices. If the answer is "no," then that is usually a clear sign that what's going on might be flirting with or even already across the line of what's not appropriate. George would be wise to focus on his left hand and remember his oath to his wife.

Digital Playground

Social media has ushered in a whole new level of pseudo intimacy. The water has gotten muddy with the level of contact people have with strangers or people from their past. The tendency is to maintain contact with people who can't or shouldn't be a part of your lives. An easy question can be asked to clear away the fog: "If I want a happy marriage and want to be fully available to my family, how is this person aiding in that?" If you can't answer that with clear certainty then the evidence speaks for itself.

Married folk are also accountable for how they present themselves. As they navigate through the dense fog of a lust-driven society, they must be mindful of what their ensemble says about them. This is no indictment on fashion but there is a difference in a man wearing a muscle shirt to go get milk because the cute chic at the store is working that shift versus it being the only clean shirt left. Take the mom at football practice who is there to support her child in his athletic activities. She may or may not be aware that three weeks ago, the coaching staff didn't have much to say to her during practice. Today, however, she and her skin-tight workout gear have given off the smell of blood in the water and the sharks are starting to circle. Suddenly they are interested in her, and not because of the sport. Suddenly her kid went from third string water boy to starting quarterback. Now, some women thrive on attention, but sometimes that attention can create a tricky situation where men will feel welcomed to make an approach. This may bring on some "eye rolling" and "whatevers" from the ladies, but we can't ignore the fact that men lust through theirs eyes and sometimes a beautiful woman with her assets on full display may cause a stir and invite inappropriate conversations. Men are not without reproach in this area, both in terms of dress and in terms of governing their eyes and, therefore, their lust. Motive is key. Men too can dress more to conquer the ladies than to make a fashion statement. This is not a wardrobe advisory book, but it's important to be aware of what's happening around you. Accountability will help to answer the question: "What do I want to wear?" Hopefully, the answer will be something that doesn't say, "Never mind this ring; I'm open to negotiations."

There are other examples of accountability that center around behaviors that indirectly affect your family, things like partying too hard and making decisions to drive home drunk. We all know too well the havoc that can be caused by car accidents or DUIs. And what about your personal habits? You are accountable to your children in regards to your health. None of us parents like the idea of someone else raising our kids, but if we have a lifestyle that lends itself to us ending up in jails or hospitals then we need to evaluate this. You need to be in a good place so you will be around later in their lives.

After School Special

Have you thought about the accountability of continuing to teach them after they come home from school? The school, TV and Internet shouldn't be the only source of education for your kids. If you frowned or sighed after reading this last statement because of the thought of not being able to relax, then hang with me for a moment. When kids get home from school they start consuming messages from everywhere; friends, TV and social media. Their world immediately becomes very noisy with influences that are louder than you and you should be the primary influence in their lives. Kids need to know the traps that the electronic world sets at their innocent feet. All kids will have their bouts with finding identity and status among their peers. It has always been like this. However the coupling of camera phones and the Internet has created a three-ring circus, open to the public. Many kids find themselves or friends online trying to out-do the latest video depicting obnoxious behavior. Unfortunately, some take it too far and lose their dignity for a lifetime as a result of those quick five minutes of fame. The accountability in our marriages extends well beyond man and wife; it encompasses our children as well.

Accountability in your child's life says, "Yes, I will read to you at night and we will eat together when possible and talk to each other so we know what is going on." It also says that there should not be a single one of your child's dreams and wishes that you don't know about.

Protect Your Investment

Accountability is a concept that is tougher than steel. It should be included in the building of all unions. When you are thoughtful of how your attitudes, decisions and actions can sometimes make you vulnerable to suspicion, infidelity, immaturity, irresponsibility and non-engagement, or appearances of the same, you can create another line of defense and protection from the multitude of things out in the world that undermine marriages. If you take on the responsibility and the initiative of creating accountability in your relationships, it not only keeps a majority of the hungry wolves at bay, it just might take your scent out of the air all together. The greatest title you can have as a married person among a circle of single people is Untouchable.

Creating Accountability: Declassified

- A relationship with no accountability is a danger to itself

- Marriage is the ultimate relationship between two people. Therefore we should give it the respect and protection it commands

- If you wouldn't do it with your spouse there in front of you, then you shouldn't do it at all

- Be mindful of what you are broadcasting to the world when you leave home

- Husbands should strive to bear responsibility for their entire family's actions through wisdom and sound judgment

- Always be aware that others are depending on you to be present in their lives

- If something isn't good for your marriage then don't engage it

- You are also accountable to your children as guardian and teacher

Chapter 16

THE SPIRITUAL BOND

When I look back at the last ten years of my life as a man of faith, I can't help but acknowledge the power and harmony in my marriage brought about by a common belief. The spiritual bond between us is broader and deeper than any label that you could put on it. This facet of our relationship has allowed us to be both jubilant and grief-stricken together, and survive some extremely stressful situations as a unit. I am not bragging on our relationship to get a high five or an Amen! I am using my own situation to highlight the overwhelming benefits and advantages of being able to go to that spiritual place with your spouse, whether it be in times of joy or pain.

The importance of spirituality in marriage is a subject that can't be exhausted or marginalized, in the sense that you should never avoid talking about it. If you and your spouse have that common thread running through your union, then you have a unique component available to you that those with a spiritual void or division don't have.

In most faiths the lead is taken by a man, with the purpose of leading his wife and children in the ways of their respective traditions. The pecking order as it has been spelled out for centuries is that the Creator has charged the husband with ultimate responsibility for understanding, demonstrating and teaching what has been revealed to him. He then passes that on to his mate and children. When this formula is followed, there is a consistency and a harmony that is achieved, and families develop a framework through which to explain the world. It is a humbling honor to be in a position to serve your family in such a manner. Since we know that men thrive on having a sense of purpose it will allow them to provide an environment in which all are respected and able to thrive.

A House Divided

A man cannot sit on the fence when it comes to such things as worshiping together, whether that be in the privacy of your own home or at a traditional church. This could be illustrated in a couple of guys at a football game in which all but one of the fanatics are shouting for the home team. This nervous individual politely excuses himself to go to the men's room but ends up on the opposite side of the stadium where he swiftly flips both his jersey and wig inside out revealing the away team's colors. He might have gotten away with the treachery but he forgot to remove the home team's #1 foam finger in that selfie he tweeted.

You've seen the family or the couple who show up at Sunday service with one of them clearly wearing the look, "I'd rather be somewhere else." That attitude does justice to neither. Nobody should be pretending to be committed to a belief or faith. Nor should anyone be pressured into doing so. It completely robs the integrity of the experience. That doesn't mean your relationship is doomed if you don't have the same values or belief system. It is, though, a realm that is meaningful, worthwhile and can usher in an undercurrent of joy.

Most of this book, as mentioned at the beginning, is a medley of experiences derived from dozens of men, including myself. To avoid speculation about who might believe what, I will focus exclusively on my personal spiritual journey and why I feel this chapter is important.

As long as I can remember I have always had a sense of something greater than myself, and through the years I have read different texts and briefly studied different faith systems in hopes of getting clarity. I have had countless discussions with people very different from myself.

The journey has been eye opening and has provided me with a fairly informed perspective of how universal messages have been communicated across the globe for centuries. What I've discovered, where it pertains to families, is a common demand for order and obedience. I stress this because I, like you, have seen the family unit in the U.S. dissolving and witness the subsequent chaotic reward. Single-parent homes are on the increase and even homes that have two parents, physically, but one of the adults has checked out. Refusing to participate is even more destructive than single parenting. It is setting an example of non-cooperation.

Sync in Progress

My wife and I see first-hand the benefits of having a framework in our home that sets expectations for behavior and responsibility. When we, and other parents of faith, can come together on a spiritual level and be of one mind then, as the saying goes, "Our joys are doubled, and our sorrows cut in half." I am sorrowful when I see people who gush at the chance to share their troubles with a stranger, when they should be taking their ills to their spouse.

My wife and I often joke about instances when we are in sync and we both notice it at the same time—things like being at work and you think about the other one, then all of a sudden the phone rings: guess who? Another example would be making a decision without the other present and the statement is made that, "I was thinking the exact same thing." We joke that we are in the fourth dimension or "4-D" when those things happen.

My spiritual calling has led down the path of Christianity and, within that, I seek the wisdom and guidance provided in biblical Scriptures. As I have grown in my faith I have begun to understand more and more about spiritual matters and how they influence us on a moment-by-moment basis. With this understanding I'm encouraging all believers to nourish this part of your relationship. It absolutely has to be a "coalition of the willing," and not one person dragging another into an environment that is neither familiar nor comfortable. Faking interest is equally unhelpful. If one of you isn't quite there yet, then exercise the principles of kindness and patience. I believe we are all wired to have a spiritual life, but it would be wise in dealing with a partner who isn't aligned with you to explain how your union can benefit from being on the same page in this regard and from there *you leave the light on for them.* This scenario would be ripe for a partner to invite the other to explore and better understand that partner's faith and how it has helped them govern their lives. The case could be made that the relationship would deepen if there was alignment here as well.

As I stated earlier, I took the long way around to understanding and exercising my faith, but it prepared me to be a better spouse and a better king in my empire. When you have been dirty and foul you can then appreciate a good hot shower and a fresh start. Whether we like it or not, we are influenced by unseen spiritual elements. It's kind of like so many of those scenes in the Matrix trilogy when the camera pans across a group of people then jumps back to the crowd and they have all morphed into agents who are now pursuing the hero. We don't know what is going on in the other dimension.

Hidden in Plain Sight

Other not-so-hidden forces are also at work—the human nature ones. When you are making a spiritual declaration within your marriage, beware that you don't fall victim to things like jealousy or patronize the vanity of others at the expense of your relationship. In a spiritual sense, *nobody* in the big old world cares if you are losing the game because that's what negativity expects. On the other hand, *everybody* cares if you are winning. Just go ahead and start having a great marriage and watch the barbarians start assembling on the hilltop. It's safe to say, generally, that the more positive things you have going on in your life, the smaller the applause from strangers. You can get anybody to go out and have a smoke or a brew if there is a chance to complain about spouses, yet few will join you in activities advancing your marriage. With this in mind, I will encourage you find support among those who want you to succeed.

Take, for example, a couple that is dealing with some medical setbacks that have put a strain on the home. The couple has an active shared belief system. With the medical crisis, tasks in the home had to be shuffled, and care for the children was affected tremendously. Parents know all too well the pressure that can build when your partner is unavailable and it's all up to you. Typically a spouse who is overburdened with responsibilities, however temporary, can be subject to varied levels of frustration and stress that can trigger a silent animosity. Fortunately for this couple, they endured their trial and are back to normal, stronger than ever. What sustained them through the ordeal was understanding that when one of you is down for the count then the other *can and must* be empowered to carry the load. If a couple reflects back on the pledge they made to each other in "sickness and health," they will be comforted through their spiritual relationship that they will be unbroken as a unit while going through the fire. This couple and others like them know for certain what a solid spiritual foundation can bring to a union. Those who stick together in tough times not only grow closer together, but they serve as examples of a solid love.

Circling the Wagons

Mentioned earlier was the importance of aligning yourself with like-minded couples as a supplemental ring of defense against exterior influences that will surely attack your relationship.

The goal of this book is to assist you in building a relationship that is **uncommon**. This kind of relationship allows you to answer the question, "How is married life treating you?" with "Like a King!" Aware or unaware, most people want to be loved unconditionally. The hard truth about reaching this goal is that the odds are stacked against you every single day when you leave the house. There is a fairly high level of pessimism about the possibility of having a great marriage, but it is all about the work you put into it—there are no short cuts or cheat codes. That is why having a spiritual foundation will help to weather the storms and celebrate victories on a deeper level. As products of your environment, survey the influences around you and ask yourself this question: *Do the values and goals with which I have surrounded myself line up with what I ultimately want from my marriage*? You can't mingle with disgruntled people and expect cheers or encouragement when you hit your own bumps in the road. This would be similar to a lion finding himself in a petting zoo with goats and chickens. The lion knows he shouldn't be there, but the others think he should lighten up and quit being a buzzkill. After some deep thought the goats realize that means more corn for them.

When you are looking at spirituality and marriage, you are both tapping into and serving something more grand and expansive than you can ever imagine. Your spiritual life will guide and protect your family as needed and, as the biblical passage goes: "Though one may be overpowered, two can defend themselves. A cord of three strands is not quickly broken." (Ecclesiastes 4:12 KJV)

With that knowledge comes a higher demand being placed on you. The accountability is heavier, but the rewards are richer as well. In no other relationship can you be *all* of you and it be okay; you can't be the razor sharp account manager who knocks every presentation out of the park and then follow it up with celebratory farting noises from your armpit without some obvious consequences. That's a daddy moment.

In essence, if your marriage is a house, then your faith is an inflatable raft in times of flooding, a private well in times of drought and a fortress when negativity comes knocking. It is a door you walk through where the "OPEN" sign never turns off. Faith is its own dimension. With it comes clarity and strength to face all the other dimensions in which we hammer out our daily lives.

The Spiritual Bond: Declassified

- We are wired for a spiritual existence, and it is most effective when fed from a common belief

- Faith should be encouraging and welcoming; if the other isn't there yet then seek to answer his or her questions and then "leave the porch light on" for him or her

- Most faith systems have a code of conduct that leads to predictable behavior and order; who couldn't use some of that?

- Men are charged with leadership not dictatorship. They are called to lead their families by example

- The spiritual bond will be the covering needed to brave some of life's toughest storms

Conclusion

SO WHY GET MARRIED?

A fair number of adults wonder why a couple should get married. What is it about marriage that is so different than just "shacking up" with someone for the rest of your days? To those who choose its path, it seems that marriage is the natural end game of falling in love and wanting to spend the rest of your life with a person. But in an era of questioning the norms, it should be looked at more deeply to try to gain a better understanding of the differences between marriage and living together.

Keep in mind that when one first decides to get married, the reasons are often different from those that keep a couple married decades later. It is part of that process you can be aware of but can't really speed up.

I chose marriage based on a special vibe that my wife had and I couldn't put my finger on it. It wasn't something that could be seen with the naked eye; it was just a "feeling." What I experienced after "surrendering" to this feeling was almost an out-of-body event where I watched myself doing and saying things I had never considered before. This event I'm trying to describe is one that most of you find yourself in when you feel pulled out of your comfort zone with a *Star Trek*-like tractor beam that carries you slowly away from the solid ground you once called home. This is what the cliché "you just know" means.

You are often pulled into marriage by that inexplicable turmoil of emotions but you slowly discover there are so many benefits that marriage provides when "used as directed." The institution of marriage can provide two major benefits that apply on a whole bunch of levels. Those benefits are Security and Purpose. Think about what it means to be secure; it's a space where you feel safe and sound. Some attributes of security are:

1. Emotionally, you can be free and unguarded with your feelings
2. Financially, you can prosper faster with two incomes
3. Sexually, you can experiment and have a focused intensity on pleasing someone who will still be there in the morning and all your mornings from there on

4. Relationally, you are with someone you know and trust rather than strangers or half strangers who once filled your life

5. Spiritually, you can unite and share a common bond through your beliefs
6. Physically, you can have the peace of companionship

These scenarios have a great deal of appeal when you are trying to conceive what married life would be like. On some level, you may be able to have those things without saying, "I do;" however, there is something different when you don't have a backdoor to run out when things get rough.

That brings us to Purpose and its attributes:

1. You leave the house every day with the knowledge that someone is depending on your efforts today

2. You benefit from the exclusivity of a love built by the two of you *for* the both of you

3. You have the sacred opportunity to raise and guide young souls through this world

4. You see the reality of who you can become by living and growing in the love being provided by someone who sees things in you that you can't see in yourself

Once you have been married for a while, you are in a position to compare what your single life provided compared to what marriage brings to the table.

In terms of what you bring to the table, I've never been one to play the lottery much, and I guess it's because I can be a little gun shy when it comes to throwing my hard earned money at a long-shot pipe dream, but looking at Las Vegas, apparently I'm in the minority.

My single life provided me with an unlimited amount of freedom: the freedom to go out on any given night and get wasted and try to bamboozle somebody equally drunk to come home with me; the freedom to sit on my couch on an autumn Saturday afternoon with the windows open and my feet in the air watching the game in complete solitude; the freedom, as well, to engage in reckless behavior without any accountability at home; and the freedom to *not* think about my future was at my disposal as well.

Absolute freedom sounds good, huh? Maybe. With this freedom also comes a loneliness and uncertainty that can keep some people awake at night. For some it means hanging out in the streets because there is no one home, no one to share victories or ease the agony of defeat. Having no one to check bad habits can leave one delusional about their personal awesomeness level. You were not designed to be alone in life. Community helps shape you. All the diamonds and all the fine pottery in the world would never exist without the heat and pressure under the earth or the calm calculating touch of the artisan at work. There has to be a yin to your yang— that someone who complements and interconnects with you—for you to be complete. To receive it though, you have to be in a position to receive it.

Picture this analogy that sprang out of a conversation with a dear friend regarding readiness for love. A man is riding in a four-door vehicle with three other passengers: ME, MYSELF and I. He is told clearly, "Think about it bro; if the love of your life wanted to come along for the ride, there would be nowhere for her to sit."

A man has to be willing to release his B.S. into the hands of someone that can heal it, and within that same gesture extend his hands that are now free to heal hers. We are all broken. Spending your days obsessing over someone's faults is like an eternal cycle of "The Blame Game," and in that contest no one ever wins.

Marriage will certainly bring out the best and worst in you, but how will you ever fix your broken pieces if you don't put them on the table to be *addressed and caressed*? How can a person who has abandonment issues ever feel safe if the "forever gesture" is never made? How can a fatherless son seize the opportunity to be the dad he never had if he never steps up to the plate and makes a genuine attempt? How can the woman with daddy issues ever understand how much she can mean to a husband if she never learns how to be the wife he needs? There are countless questions to be asked about a love deferred because of fear, doubt and guilt, but the answer lies within a rock solid commitment between two souls who have some sense of what they can have together if they only honor and respect the vow and oath they will have taken as a unit.

In my short thirty-six years on this earth I have learned a multitude of lessons and as a result have gained wisdom to make my walk a little smoother. One of my favorites is that I am indeed valuable and I experience joy when I am mindful of this, but it is not at the expense of other people's amazingness.

There is great reward in confronting adversity backed by a love that greatly overshadows the problem at hand. Out of this comes a capacity for compassion and understanding that you can't gain anywhere else. I cannot say emphatically enough that I believe most people can have extraordinary marriages, but it will require extraordinary efforts from both sides to generate that harmony and circulate it through the relationship.

Anyone who tells you that marriages don't have problems is selling you a dream. **Yes,** there will be nights when you turn your backs on each other in bed, but after that comes love. **Yes,** there will be decisions that require your input regardless of whether you give a damn or not, but after that comes love. **Yes,** there will be days when you want to disappear after a rough day with the baby, but after that comes love. **Yes,** you may have to come home early from a guy's night out, but what's waiting on you is love. **No,** you cannot see what else is out there because what you will find *is not love.* **No,** you can't just give up and quit in the face of difficulty because who then will maintain the love?

There is no razzle-dazzle in matrimony, just a simple exchange of work and reward. Put little to no love in what you do and that's what's coming out the other end. If you completely throw yourself into this relationship then what you should expect and deserve is the very same thing.

My name is Michael Warren, and I gave up the gamesmanship, lies and chaos in order to gain certainty, truth and harmony.

My last question is: Will you?

THE *MARRIAGE* DECLASSIFIED FIELD TRAINING GUIDE

The following information is intended to promote thoughtful conversations and assist readers with a level of self-discovery that can open up a clearer path to a meaningful marriage. Please take the time to reflect and process the information in an honest manner. The integrity of this next experience will rely on your full participation. I hope that you are moved to action within your own relationships.

Chapter 1

YOU MATTER

One of the most critical concepts we should share in a marriage is that both people understand that they are desired in many different ways and that they have strong value in the relationship. Our worlds can be very noisy and chaotic at times. People continue to overschedule themselves and find themselves bound to a high-speed routine of responsibilities at work and at home. In this environment where everyone is playing out a role in this feature film that we call our lives it can be easy to lose sight of each other. Particularly on an emotional level. It is imperative that spouses establish and maintain a regiment of ensuring their partner doesn't fade into the background. Below are some questions that can help understand where you currently are and highlight any opportunities to get better.

Answer the following questions:

1. When you hear that "you matter" what does it mean to you?
2. How does your partner matter to you?
3. What are ways that you show them that they are important?
4. How often do you verbally tell her that they she is important?
5. What gestures could be either increased or improved upon?

Suggested actions:

- Write a letter to your partner indicating why you are valuable and how that benefits the relationship

- Also include why your partner matters to you and give examples of how you can further demonstrate it to them

Chapter 2
LET'S WAKE UP AND CATCH UP

It is safe to assume that most adults have inherited a world much different than the one their parents were raised in. The reasons can vary, whether it be cultural shifts brought on by new ideas or advances in technology. In current times we experience the latter. A child born in the late '70s grew up with only three channels on TV. That child's parents grew up with no TV at all, and the generation prior to them may not have had electricity at all. The point is that times change, and if you aren't aware of shifts in your world, you may find yourself swallowed up by them. It is important for couples to understand their world and how it affects their relationship as well as the notion that children may come along at some point. There can be situations where an "old school" approach to life is warranted, but the adverse of this is equally true if we base our ideology on what's useful to our marriage.

Answer the following questions:

1. What are some of the biggest changes you have experienced in your world that you think affect relationships?

2. What sorts of things do you think are *helpful* to relationships?

3. What sorts of things do you think are *harmful* to relationships?

4. What will your roles as spouses be on an average day?

5. What will the foundation of your marriage be based upon?

6. Are there any differences in your worldviews?

Suggested actions:

- Make time to discuss how your relationship is affected by societal trends

- If there are any adverse effects, then attempt to address them in a constructive manner

Chapter 3
MAN ABANDONED

In *Marriage Declassified* we established that men will abandon their own dreams and desires in order to fulfill the wishes and expectations of others. While this may be necessary at times to get through one of life's seasons it should not spell out the death of a man's dreams or the un-tapping of his inner potential. There lies within all of us a special gift or ability regardless of gender or geography. We have all seen or heard of people who had a gift and never pursued it or didn't have guidance to channel it in a healthy direction. Men can find a deeper sense of purpose and fulfillment when they discover the things that resonate with them, whether it be something mechanical or organic. Take the time to discover or recover any dreams or ambitions not yet realized and figure out how to make them a part of your life.

Answer the following questions:
1. What kinds of ambitions have you had in the past?
2. What success have you had with pursuing them?
3. Does your partner know about them?
4. How can your partner help you with realizing your gifts?
5. What would your dream job or hobby be?

Suggested actions:
- Make time to identify what your gifts or talents are and either share them or revisit them with your partner

- Discuss what their level of importance is to you. Evaluate how and when you can make time to develop them

- Once it has been established that there are no threats to existing responsibilities then you can agree on steps to move forward

Chapter 4

THE ENGAGEMENT PERIOD, BLOWN OPPORTUNITY

Proposing marriage to someone is a monumental gesture. The wave of thoughts and emotions can be both overwhelming and intoxicating when you are choosing someone to potentially build a life with. The engagement period is the perfect time to figure out how to work together and assess what each other's strengths and weaknesses are in regards to teamwork. This phase is typically a rollercoaster ride for the bride and her family because of all of the things that need to be coordinated in order to pull off the "perfect day." Men have an opportunity to find out how they can be helpful during this time in an effort to see what future endeavors will be like when your input will be appreciated even if a groom is indifferent to the outcome.

Pre-marital counseling can't be underestimated in its importance. It should bring to light all facets of marital life. Take care not to rush this process because this experience can and should prompt some tough conversations that may reveal things not previously seen or considered.

Compromise is a balancing act that you must get proficient in. There will always be scenarios that will pit an individual's wants against the needs of the union. It is paramount that a couple not let ego or entitlement cloud their view of what is most important.

Answer the following questions:
1. What was your motivation for proposing?
2. How can you be more involved in the wedding planning?
3. What sorts of things make the two of you a good team?
4. What do you hope to get out of counseling?
5. How do you make compromises?
6. What are some tough issues you would want answers to?

Suggested actions:
- Seek out good counsel from a third party that can both educate you and help give unbiased advice for any concerns that may arise
- Have discussions about what compromises each of you are willing or unwilling to make in your marriage

Chapter 5
SOBERING REALITY

There will come a point in the early stages of marriage when a guy will ask himself "What have I gotten myself into?" The answer to this was one of the main drivers for writing the book. The short answer is that it is the ultimate relationship that has the potential to change your life. The direction of this change all depends on how much work you are willing to put into it. Men will typically not have an idea of what is expected of them early on and that reality can lead to some discouraging failures and disappointments. New husbands can benefit from aligning themselves with other husbands who are experienced and have a healthy marriage. These resources will be invaluable when the first waves of conflict and confusion come your way. Learning how to sacrifice certain things and prioritize your marriage early on will pay dividends down the road. The perception of giving up some of the minor things for the greater good is an easier experience than feeling like you are being robbed of something.

Negotiating new family ties is always tricky and can take time. Some husbands experience a quick assimilation into the family and others are still calling their father-in-law "Mr. So and So" after five years. No matter what your pace is the goal is that there exist a healthy respect that will hopefully lead to a deeper connection. In some situations it will be up to the bride or even the groom to express the importance of this person being included into the family without too much static. Ultimately both families just want their loved ones to be happy. The other goal is to establish some boundaries for both families to respect that allow time for the new couple to figure out their new normal. New routines can't take root and flourish if family members are at your house several times a week. That boundary is difficult to put in place, but it is so worth it.

Answer the following questions:
1. At what point did the reality of marriage hit you?
2. Did you foresee any changes?
3. What do you wish you had known early on?
4. Who will you turn to when you need advice? Why?
5. Marriage is hard work, but do you know why?
6. Sacrifice is necessary. What are you willing to sacrifice in this new relationship?
7. What is your spouse willing to sacrifice?
8. What is your relationship like with your in-laws?

Suggested actions:
- Establish relationships with a sacred few whom you trust with being available to advise you and hold you accountable when adversity comes into the picture

- Discuss what you are willing to sacrifice for your marriage and how you think it will help your relationship evolve

- Share what your current status in the new family is and what your expectations are going forward

- Include how your spouse can help usher that in if necessary

Chapter 6

THE TRUST BUCKET

Trust is the most critical component of your marriage. It is like an underground river system that gives water to the plants on the surface. No matter if you are a patch of moss or a towering pine tree, you get your sustenance from that flow. With this in mind we need to understand how this plays out in our relationships. Having the complete trust of another can be a rewarding and empowering feeling. Not having that trust can make for a complex existence. Trust is also very fragile and difficult to restore once broken. It is as if the above mentioned river were polluted somehow and now requires an extensive cleanup process to regain its original integrity. Couples can thrive in all areas of their marriage if their trust in each other provides safety and peace of mind.

Answer the following questions:

1. What is your current understanding of how trust plays into relationships?
2. What is your spouse trusting you with now?
3. What are you not being trusted with?
4. What would you like to be trusted with?
5. How do you deal with broken trust?
6. What ways can you protect trust in the future?

Suggested actions:

- Facilitate a discussion with your spouse about what trust means to your relationship

- Explain why you can trust your spouse

- Ask some open ended questions about how you can be better trusted

- If either of you have experienced broken trust then explain what happened and how you recovered from it

Chapter 7
WHERE THE HELL DID MY GIRLFRIEND GO?

When we ask the above question it becomes very telling about some of the differences in perspective between spouses. They can certainly bring about some confusion. In an effort to clear things up we should strive to understand a bigger plan being in play that we need to be a part of. While your average guy will be satisfied with the **now**, she may already be thinking about 5 years from **now**. The opportunity for men lies in comprehending and owning the idea that their leadership and participation in a different scenario will be optimal.

Your wife will be focused on building a nest for the family and you will be expected to help bring in the twigs. This change in priorities from hanging out and making out to planning ahead and living long is necessary and a lot easier to digest when you know the reason why. So now that you know where your girlfriend went, hurry up and catch her.

Answer the following questions:
1. What did you love about your then girlfriend?
2. Are any of those traits still there?
3. How many of your future plans are being realized?
4. What activities have been carried over from when you were dating?
5. What changes in lifestyle need to happen for long term happiness?

6. Where would your wife say that your girlfriend went?

Suggested actions:

- Review your time as girlfriend and boyfriend and discuss what you both enjoyed about that time and figure out if there was anything lost that might still be useful or possible in the new marriage setting

- Should anything come to mind then work together to figure out how to usher that thing back into your lives

Chapter 8

AGGRESSIVE DEBATES, A.K.A. ARGUING

We should all understand by now that as long as there are two people on this earth there will be a conflict or difference in perspective. This has and always will lead to some sort of friction. When emotions are included then that friction ignites a fire and if that fire isn't contained or addressed then it erupts into a raging inferno that may be hard to recover from.

When arguments erupt and emotions spin out of control there has to be someone to drop anchor and stay steady in order to see and hear what the real problems are. The silver bullet for assumptions is a direct and honest question. Real and meaningful changes can only happen when clear goals are set and proper steps to get there are laid out. Consistent engagement keeps the communication lines open and allows for opportunities for all to be heard and sets us all up to deal with the little fires and not shocked by the big ones. Harnessing the power of the "state of the union" letters will aid in this.

A difficult but useful skill to develop is the ability to hold fast during an argument and then begin walking closer instead of away. The goal is never to **win** the argument but to **solve** the argument.

Answer the following questions:
1. When is the best time to bring you bad news?
2. How do you currently handle conflict and what is the outcome?

3. How can you communicate better?

4. How can you show your spouse that you understand them during an argument?

5. How often do you and your partner check on each other's emotions?

6. If you implemented the State of the Union Letter process, what would be the impact?

Suggested actions:

- When things are cool, discuss with your partner what each of your triggers are for an argument

- Make a declaration to each other that you will strive to not react adversely when conflict arises in order to get true understanding about an issue

- Develop a habit of checking in on each other on a weekly basis

- Implement the state of the union letter process

Chapter 9
HUSBAND OR DO BOY

The idea of anyone being or feeling like an indentured servant is archaic and has no place in today's relationships. The truth of the matter is that we all have lots of things to bring to the table. Men have typically been at the heart of "getting it done" in most settings both personal and professional. In today's environment we are blessed to include the labor and insight of our women as well. Things move very fast today and it is very easy to overschedule ourselves which may lead to an overuse of delegation powers. There will always be things to do and chase but the primary target should be your spouse.

Partnership is the key in today's marriages. Both people should understand the other person's value and contributions in the relationship. Emphasizing teamwork and an appreciation for the work that is in front of a couple leads to efficiencies that translate into other facets of the marriage. Nobody can do it all, nor should they have to.

Answer the following questions:

1. Have you ever felt like a "Do Boy"?
2. How do you define being a husband?
3. What is the philosophy in your home regarding who does a particular thing?
4. How much time do currently leave open as "free time"?
5. What things are you not included in that you would like to be?
6. Do you consider your spouse to be a "Battle-Buddy? Why or why not?

Suggested actions:

- Define for yourself the type of husband you want to be and communicate that to your wife

- Explain what your intentions are for her and the family

- If there are feelings of being overburdened or overscheduled, then discuss and understand what parts of that are necessary and those that are not useful

- Discuss what your roles are in an effective partnership

- If your lifestyle is fast paced then plan for a calculated slow down periodically

Chapter 10

OUR MONEY

Finances have and will always play a significant role in marriage. With this knowledge, couples need to understand and develop a vision for their financial goals. It is probably safe to assume that in most marriages there is a spender and a saver who may be potentially working against each other. One partner may have the philosophy that tomorrow isn't promised, so have your fun today, While another may say "yeah, but if tomorrow does come then we are in deep trouble."

Discussions about money can get very uncomfortable quickly, because for most of us it symbolizes our security and ability to be mobile in life. Any threat to this can bring out a less than sunny part of ourselves. To help diminish any concerns in this area, you will want to have the same philosophy about money and be able to have healthy dialogue about its use in any given situation. When you are building a life with your partner, it's important to be collectively working towards your financial goals and prioritize them over individual yearnings for "stuff."

As a unit, you are jointly responsible for your financial situation. Whomever brings home the bulk of the money does not automatically gain infallible omnipotence when it comes to making decisions about how the money is spent. The more disposable income that is available, the greater the desire for things that are momentary at best. The best plan for your money is that your money be planned for. There are enough models available to us that demonstrate that if you save early and often you can weather the storms that lie in waiting. So work hard and have money, but don't let money have you.

Answer the following questions:

1. What is your history with money?
2. Are you a spender or a saver?
3. What are your spouse's spending habits?
4. How much money do you need to feel financially safe? What is your partner's number?

5. What are your budgetary practices?
6. Who earns the most money? Is that important to you?
7. How would your behavior change if you inherited a large sum of money?

Suggested actions:

- Make a pledge to have regular meetings about your financial health

- Understand both of your spending habits
- Hold each other accountable for irresponsible behavior

- Educate yourself about how to make your money work for you

- Strive to remain grounded and not lose yourself in money matters

Chapter 11
SEX AND ROMANCE

Sex and Romance are much like the process that cause volcanoes to erupt. If sex is the eruption we see with our eyes then romance is the lava flowing underneath that builds the pressure. In a marriage there is need for both in ample doses. Where there is a mutual effort to keep romance alive in the relationship a couple can expect to find what they seek which is love and yes sex as well.

All spouses want to feel desirable not only physically but emotionally. With this in mind, we must own the idea that we should continue to pursue each other romantically. Frequent reminders that she still does it for you or that there is no one else out there goes a long way towards a great love life.

We all chose our wives when we proposed marriage, so let us continue to "choose" them in all the ways that they enrich our lives.

Answer the following questions:
1. How big of a role does both sex and romance play in your particular marriage?
2. How often do you expect sexual intimacy?
3. How often can your wife expect romance?
4. When was the last time either of you professed your love for the other?
5. What ways do you show that you desire your spouse?
6. What ways would you like to be shown that you are desirable?

Suggested actions:
- Have a healthy conversation about your sex life without any assumptions or preconceived notions

- Explain what you enjoy now or would enjoy in the future

- Evaluate the ways that both of you communicate your desire for each other

- Set realistic expectations for frequency in sex and romantic encounters as well

- Make time to be intimately engaged but not sexual

- Make declarations to each other about what you enjoy the most about her

Chapter 12

FATHERHOOD

The principle of Fatherhood is in play in every level of the family. Its importance can't be understated because it brings with it the demands of Leadership and Ultimate Responsibility. A Father is charged with guiding his entire family along life's road with all its twist and turns. Even in this role, the father himself needs fathering from an elder or someone who is much more wise and experienced.

Fathers are at the service of their family. It is a noble and rewarding existence, but it does require sacrifice. Oddly enough, a father is the resident Fire Department, E.M.S. and S.W.A.T. team. Whatever situation pops up he has to be ready to handle it regardless if the game is on or not. He will be more effective if he stays engaged with his family to understand exactly what they need from him. This is done through constant communication and quality time spent together. As a father knows his family, he should also know himself and what he needs to remain effective in this part of his life. It is imperative that he have an outlet or periodic moments to reflect and rejuvenate lest he find himself "burned out" and therefore less effective over time.

A father can find purpose and validation in the achievements of his children, the allegiance of his wife and the overall prosperity of a household built on trust, guided by wisdom and powered by a love much greater than his own. Fathering is a tough job, but don't worry you were built for it.

Answer the following questions:
1. What does fatherhood mean to you?
2. What kind of Dad do you want to be?
3. Who is your model for fatherhood?
4. What fears do you have about fathering?
5. What is your vision for your family?
6. What sacrifices are you willing to make to be a better father?

Suggested actions:
- If you have children, discuss with them what your responsibility to them is

- Establish your vision for fathering your children

- Align yourself with other fathers to develop a support network

- Be sure to find a responsible way to rejuvenate periodically

- When things get rough, remember that you are capable, necessary and no one else can do it like you do

Chapter 13

KIDS, AND THEN THERE WERE THREE

Children represent so many things in our lives. Everything from the embodiment of the pure things in life to the promise of a better tomorrow. With this in mind we should all appreciate that it is our actions that brought them into this world and so we have the responsibility in providing for them a safe and healthy environment to flourish in.

Kids will demand all of your attention and resources in order for them to be setup for success. This requirement can cause a divide 2 miles wide between husband and wife as they adjust into being mommy and daddy. You have to be clever and resourceful in maintaining your "original love." It will need to be on full display four children to see how a man is supposed to treat a woman and how a she is supposed to treat her man. It is their Relationship 101 class on day one. Don't lose sight of each other and check in regularly.

A child's needs will vary as they grow from infant to young adults, but there are some roots that never change. Those roots are called *time* and *attention*. Consider being dropped on an alien planet where you know nothing about language, geography or customs, all you know is what you see. Take the time to teach and demonstrate to them what they should know. Also give them your attention and patience while those same things develop. They are empty vessels when they come to us, so commit to "pouring into them" because if you don't, *someone* or *something* else will.

You will know true pride and joy as you watch your children grow, discover and explore the world. Your unconditional love will give them the wings they need to catch the wind and soar off into the sunset. We can only hope and pray that they use the map and compass we've given them.

Answer the following questions:

1. How can you and your wife keep your relationship intact during child rearing years?

2. How can you demonstrate a healthy relationship for your kids to see?
3. How do you show love? Is it adequate for those around you?
4. What ways can you be more patient?
5. Are you prepared to be your child's teacher?

Suggested actions:

- Create time to keep your relationship with your wife fresh and engaged

- Be mindful of what you demonstrate at home without saying anything

- Never miss an opportunity to explain something to your children

- Know what you represent to your kids through their eyes

- Patience, patience and more patience

Chapter 14

THE HALL OF "DON'T BOTHER ME"

The world we live in is extremely noisy and full of distractions. It seems that our collective attention spans have become shorter and shorter over the years. It has become increasingly more important to find ways to decompress and quiet our minds and the environment around us.

Overtime, men have found different ways to find a slice of solitude in some form or another. After dealing with the demands of work and preparing for the ones waiting at home they will benefit from a brief pause in order to change gears.

These "Zen moments," or whatever you want to call them, should be devoted to decompressing from the work day and making sure that any stress from the job is left at the front door and not brought inside with you where it will surely look for a new resting place via the wife or kids, and that's not right.

The Hall should be occupied mostly for therapeutic purposes and not serve as a hideout from any responsibilities or to be unavailable when the family has a legitimate need. The goal of having this space or time set aside for Dad or Hubby is for him to assume an effective posture in the home and be ready to serve his family with a sober spirit.

It should be noted that the Hall is for men, but there does exist a parallel equivalent for the wife. A wise man would find out what and where that is. If it doesn't exist then add that to your "Honey Do" list.

In today's environment it is typical that couples both work and have their share of demands on their time. The idea here is that we need time to not bring the world into the last refuge we have and that is our homes and our family's love.

Answer the following questions:
1. How do you currently decompress from your day?
2. What obstacles stand in your way of changing gears, if any?
3. Based on your household, how much time is realistic to be *unplugged* while you gather yourself?

4. How does your wife unwind?
5. What ways can you and your wife ensure periods of solitude for each other?

Suggested actions:
- Evaluate how you currently "get the day off of you" and if that is impairing your availability to your home

- Explore your daily routines for the home and find new efficiencies to possibly free up time

- Consider having no TV for few days in order to see how much time is actually available for other things

- Discuss with your wife what her needs are and figure out how to help her find her own "hall"

Chapter 15

CREATING ACCOUNTABILITY

Every governing body, whether it be public or private has some sort of system of checks and balances to protect the integrity of its original purpose. Our relationships are no different in that we benefit from the good things that come from our bond with one another and we don't want that to be compromised by outside influences or general foolishness. Creating accountability ensures that you have set expectations for behaviors and habits that are conducive to the health of your relationship. If you have a job to go to in the morning or a family who depends on your income, then it probably doesn't make sense to be getting locked up for DUI or picking fights in a parking lot.

Accountability also comes in the form of aligning yourself with like-minded couples who are in a good place, because the hope is that someone will pull you aside and encourage you to do better if you're out of line or have lost your way. Making declarations to those important to you also writes a contract with terms into the hearts and minds of those cherished few who reserve the right to call foul. A commitment to always being truthful regardless of the consequences places accountability because behaving in a dishonest manner will be immediately recognized. There are tons of influences in the world that will try to lead you off the path of harmony with your family. It takes a lot of courage to walk away from trouble and even more guts to make a sound decision when it isn't popular, but that is just the kind of hero our families need.

Answer the following questions:
1. Who are you accountable to now?
2. What opportunities do you have to govern yourself better?
3. Does your family understand what their level of accountability to each other is?
4. What is the best way you can demonstrate the accountability principle for your loved ones?

Suggested actions:
- Make time to create a list of people that depend on you to be at your best

- Think about how you conduct yourself now and assess if any of your behavior is negatively impacting your loved ones

- Have the courage to admit any faults and make a declaration to evolve, along with accountability that helps you succeed

- Surround yourself with people to hold themselves accountable in a healthy manner

Chapter 16

THE SPIRITUAL CONNECTION

A person's faith will always be a sensitive topic of discussion because it is the place from which they draw hope, inspiration and peace. A person who has a spiritual life will need someone to share in that experience. Married couples who share the same faith have a unique relationship in that they can be united in times of joy and pain. This unity will be critical as children start to arrive on the scene because they will need to hear and see a consistent theme when it comes to explaining the world. They will also need a moral compass to follow and if there is a spiritual division in the home, then it makes for some impossible conversations down the road that will ultimately leave some hurt feelings and confusion.

Historically, men have been charged with leading the household in most matters and the spiritual realm is no different. A husband will benefit himself and his family tremendously if he strives to educate and empower himself in spiritual matters. The family will be looking to him for guidance and comfort when tough times come knocking at the door. The ability to perform in this role for your loved ones will go miles and miles in the way of securing your family's trust.

A couple who are synchronized in spiritual matters will have a unique existence within each other's hearts. This connection not only serves them, but also for other couples who just may not be collectively "there yet." It is absolutely true that iron sharpens iron, so once a couple have united themselves in the spirit and have their torch burning bright, they can lean over and light the wick of another couple. Just imagine.

Answer the following questions:

1. What views do you and your wife share about your spiritual life?
2. How are you as a couple, currently expressing your spirituality?
3. Are there any opportunities to strengthen this area of your life?
4. How are you managing any differences?
5. What would a new focus on this area bring to your family?

Suggested actions:

- Discuss the importance of your faith together

- Come to an agreement on how spiritual matters will be managed in your home

- Be proactive about discovering ways to deepen your connection

- Make a pledge to be prayerful and patient with any current divides